What if Carthage Won the Punic Wars? An Alternative History of the Conflict Between Rome and Carthage

By Charles River Editors

A depiction of Hannibal crossing the Alps during the Second Punic War

Charles River Editors is a boutique digital publishing company, specializing in bringing history back to life with educational and engaging books on a wide range of topics. Keep up to date with our new and free offerings with this 5 second sign up on our weekly mailing list, and visit Our Kindle Author Page to see other recently published Kindle titles.

We make these books for you and always want to know our readers' opinions, so we encourage you to leave reviews and look forward to publishing new and exciting titles each week.

Introduction

An ancient mosaic depicting a Carthaginian trireme

"Ceterum autem censeo Carthaginem esse delendam." ("Furthermore, I consider it imperative that Carthage be destroyed.") - Cato the Elder

According to Roman legend, the father of the Roman people was a Trojan by the name of Aeneas. When the Greeks broke into the city of Troy with the aid of their wooden decoy horse, Aeneas escaped the sack and burning of his home city along with a group of followers. In an epic journey modeled on that of Odysseus's journey in Homer's *Odyssey*, they wandered the seas for seven years before washing ashore in northern Africa after a storm. They landed in Carthage, the most powerful city in the region, lying on the promontory that now houses modern day Tunis. There, Aeneas met Dido, the beautiful, independent queen of Carthage. Dido had sworn off love, but she was captivated by Aeneas, and he was equally intrigued by her. They became lovers, and a year later Dido suggested marriage.

Ultimately, however, Aeneas was convinced that his destiny lay beyond the walls of Carthage and the shores of Africa. He stole away with his men and ships in the night. When Dido discovered that he was gone, she fell into despair. With a fervent prayer that her death should haunt Aeneas and his descendants, she fell on her own sword, and with that she sealed a curse that doomed Carthage and Rome to permanent enmity.

Whatever the truth behind the legends, Rome and Carthage rarely could maintain peace after the end of the 4th century BCE. As the two most powerful civilizations in the western Mediterranean, they were destined to clash, curse or not.

Roman historians placed the foundation of Carthage at approximately 814 BCE, several decades before Rome. The settlers of Carthage were of Phoenician descent, tracing their ancestry back to the great city of Tyre on the southern coast of Lebanon, but Carthage soon transformed from a minor Phoenician colony into the capital of its own growing civilization. The city itself was well positioned for shipping, and it soon dominated maritime trade. Along with that, the Carthaginians built a powerful and well-trained navy, whose protection, combined with its strategic location, made the city of Carthage a formidable prospect to attack. At its height, Carthage housed several hundred thousand inhabitants, living under a republican governmental system operated by the Carthaginian Senate. As Carthage grew, it began to expand, conquering by sea and establishing new colonies to improve trade networks. One of the Carthaginians' key objectives was Sicily.

Meanwhile, Rome's foundations came some decades after Carthage, the traditional date falling on April 21, 753 BCE. Like Carthage, Rome soon rearranged her governmental system into a Republic, with the majority of political power housed in the Senate which was led by two consuls who held yearly offices. Though situated on the Italian Peninsula, Rome itself sat inland. Trade was slower to develop in Rome than in Carthage, and a strong navy was never as vital to the security of the city. Instead, Rome developed an exemplary army, one with far more tactical flexibility than any that had come before. With this army, and a certain natural tenacity, the Romans quickly began to spread and conquer, taking city by city and nation by nation until, by the beginning of the third century BCE, she had taken control of the entire Italian Peninsula. Carthage was one of the great ancient civilizations, and at its peak, the wealthy Carthaginian Empire dominated the Mediterranean against the likes of Greece and Rome, with commercial enterprises and influence stretching from Spain to Turkey. In fact, at several points in history it had a very real chance of replacing the fledgling Roman empire or the failing Greek city-states altogether as master of the Mediterranean. Although Carthage by far preferred to exert economic pressure and influence before resorting to direct military power (and even went so far as to rely primarily on mercenary armies paid with its vast wealth for much of its history), it nonetheless produced a number of outstanding generals, from the likes of Hanno Magnus to the great bogeyman of Roman nightmares himself: Hannibal.

Certain foreign policy decisions led to continuing enmity between Carthage and the burgeoning power of Rome, and what followed was a series of wars which turned from a battle for Mediterranean hegemony into an all-out struggle for survival. Although the Romans gained the upper hand in the wake of the First Punic War, Hannibal brought the Romans to their knees for over a decade during the Second Punic War. While military historians are still amazed that he was able to maintain his army in Italy near Rome for nearly 15 years, scholars are still puzzled over some of his decisions, including why he never attempted to march on Rome in the first place.

After the serious threat Hannibal posed during the Second Punic War, the Romans didn't wait much longer to take the fight to the Carthaginians in the Third Punic War, which ended with Roman legions smashing Carthage to rubble. As legend has it, the Romans literally salted the ground upon which Carthage stood to ensure its destruction once and for all. Despite having a major influence on the Mediterranean for nearly five centuries, little evidence of Carthage's past might survives. The city itself was reduced to nothing by the Romans, who sought to erase all physical evidence of its existence, and though its ruins have been excavated, they have not provided anywhere near the wealth of archaeological items or evidence as ancient locations like Rome, Athens, Syracuse, or even Troy. Today, Carthage is a largely unremarkable suburb of the city of Tunis, and though there are some impressive ancient monuments there for tourists to explore, the large majority of these are the result of later Roman settlement.

The Punic Wars spanned more than a century, brought the loss of approximately 400,000 lives, and eventually led to the utter defeat and destruction of Carthage, but it was no easy victory for Rome, and on several occasions the young Roman Republic was close to annihilation. Given what happened in the wake of the Punic Wars, historians have long been left to ponder what might have happened had the Carthaginians won, especially given how close Hannibal came to accomplishing such a victory against Rome during the Second Punic War. *What if Carthage Won the Punic Wars? An Alternative History of the Conflict Between Rome and Carthage* profiles the conflict and examines how events may have gone quite differently for Europe if Rome had been defeated.

Growing Tensions

Though the ancient historians, basing their accounts on mythological theories, argued that Carthage was founded around 1250 BCE, modern archaeological exploration suggests that a figure of circa 850 BC is more correct. Perhaps the most famous ancient myth in circulation was that Queen Elissar, better known as Queen Dido, founded Carthage. This found currency among both Greek and Roman sources. In his famous text *Geography*, Strabo wrote:

> "Carthage is situated upon a peninsula, comprising a circuit of 360 stadia, with a wall, of which sixty stadia in length are upon the neck of the peninsula, and reach from sea to sea. Here the Carthaginians kept their elephants, it being a wide open place. In the middle of the city was the acropolis, which they called Byrsa, a hill of tolerable height with dwellings round it. On the summit was the temple of Esculapius, which was destroyed when the wife of Asdrubas burnt herself to death there, on the capture of the city. Below the Acropolis were the harbors and the Cothon, a circular island, surrounded by a canal communicating with the sea (Euripus), and on every side of it (upon the canal) were situated sheds for vessels.

> Carthage was founded by Dido, who brought her people from Tyre. Both this colony and the settlements in Spain and beyond the Pillars proved so successful to the Phoenicians, that even to the present day they occupy the best parts on the continent of Europe and the neighboring islands. They obtained possession of the whole of Africa, with the exception of such parts as could only be held by nomad tribes. From the power they acquired they raised a city to rival Rome…"

Carthage was almost certainly founded during the colonization boom of the Phoenician Empire. This was a movement which took advantage of the relative collapse in the fortunes of Greece, Crete and the Hittite Empire to establish a string of up to 3,000 colonies between Asia Minor and Spain, and Carthage was conveniently positioned smack in the middle of the extremely lucrative Iberia–Asia Minor raw metals route. Although it was a convenient position, Carthage itself was apparently not intended to be anything special in terms of colonizing efforts, particularly because the Phoenician colonial method differed radically from the Greek variant. While the Hellenes would create a settlement that was self-sustaining and almost always self-governing, while still retaining ties of alliance and friendship with the so-called "Mother City" on mainland Greece, the Phoenicians, both for administrative control reasons and due to population constraints, did not as a rule create self-sufficient colonies. Instead, the Phoenicians exerted more control over the settlements, particularly when it came to trade regulations. Thus, the settlement which gradually spread upon the hill of Byrsa was very low in the food chain.

From 850–650 BCE, Carthage gradually became more and more wealthy thanks to her privileged position straddling the major land and sea trade routes of the Mediterranean. These two centuries saw the emergence of what would later become known as "Punic" (Carthaginian) culture, a distinctly West African Phoenician identity which differed noticeably from its predecessor. The growth of this culture indicated a rise in influence on Carthage's part, and that rise manifested itself in 650 BCE when Carthage founded its own independent colony, a settlement on Ibiza, without assistance from Tyre. As the fortunes of Tyre and the Phoenician Empire waned, first with the loss of Sicily to the ever-expanding Greeks and then with Nebuchadnezzar of Babylon's great siege of Tyre in 585 BCE, Carthage's fortunes continued to rise. More settlements were founded, more cities of the North African seaboard were brought under direct Carthaginian control rather than paying their dues to Tyre, and a large colony was established in Syrtis, between Tunisia and Lybia. Additionally, Carthage's rise was bolstered by the influx of a large number of immigrants of both wealth and high political status from Tyre itself, as many of the elite fled the conflicts which enveloped the Phoenician capital.

For centuries, Carthage's expansion had progressed relatively smoothly, with no one challenging their dominion over the Mediterranean. Even the Etruscans, whose heyday coincided with Carthage's rise to prominence, had not vied with the Punic Empire for supremacy. In fact, the Etruscans had become valued trading partners and then allies, despite several incidents involving pirates.

However, near the end of the 6th century, a new power was emerging on the Mediterranean with hitherto unseen forcefulness, swallowing up the Etruscan cities and pursuing a policy of ruthless military expansion which threatened to upset the balance of power for good. The Carthaginian elite felt nervous enough watching the rapid growth of Rome that in 509 BCE, a treaty, the first of several, was signed between Carthage and Rome. Although at the time Carthage was far more significant both politically and militarily, an ally on the Italian mainland who would be both belligerent and at odds with the Greeks was certainly useful. The treaty itself was similar to others that the Carthaginians had signed with various states throughout the Mediterranean, and it served to limit the sphere of influence and commercial enterprise each power was meant to abide by.

In 348, Carthage signed another treaty with Rome, which was now quickly becoming the dominant power in Italy. Rome gained trade access (but not settlement rights) to Sicily, while Carthage maintained a monopoly on trade in Iberia and Sardinia. Rome also gained valuable Latin possessions from the treaty, further cementing its position as a dominant Italian power.

This initially cordial relationship, however, would prove to be far from lasting. Inevitably, Carthage and Rome would be locked in a mortal struggle that would define one city and ruin the other.

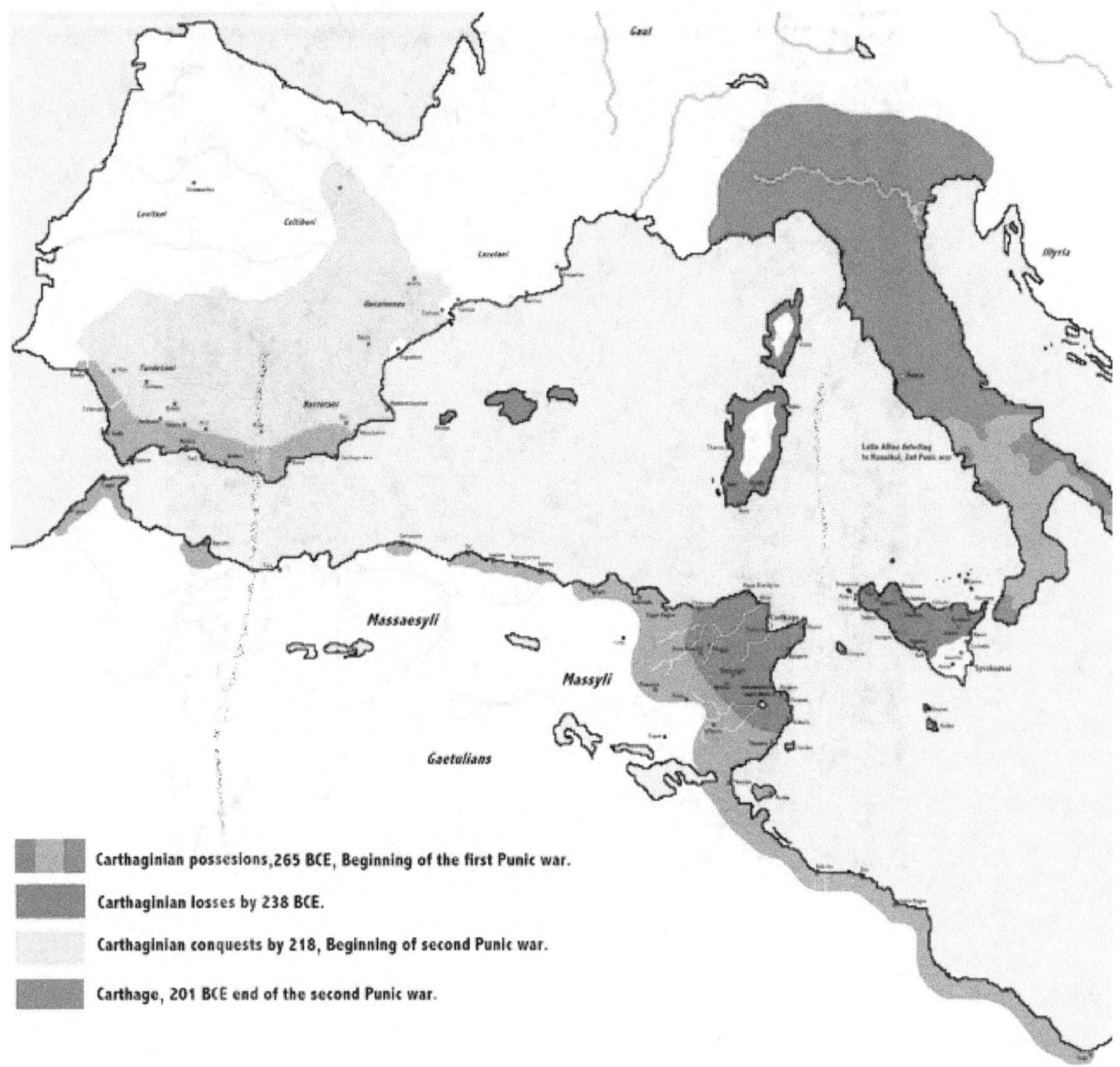

Map of the Carthaginian Empire during the 3rd century BCE

Sicily was largely at peace, barring the occasional skirmish, for several decades after the peace with Agathocles, but Carthage had plenty of internal and external threats to worry about, not least the burgeoning power of Rome, despite their peace treaty (another treaty was allegedly signed in 306 BC, but its authenticity is questionable). Sicily was not a problem again until around 280, when Carthage launched a renewed attack on the Sicilian city-states, seizing Akragas and besieging Syracuse. Pyrrhus, King of Epirus, was busy waging war against the Roman Republic in Southern Italy when he received a request for aid from several Sicilian *poleis*, Syracuse among them, against Carthage.

Ancient bust of Pyrrhus

Pyrrhus sailed for Sicily with a vast army, forcing Mago, the Carthaginian general, to lift the siege of Syracuse. Pyrrhus then captured Eryx and demanded that Carthage quit the island of Sicily entirely. When these terms were refused, he once again defeated the Carthaginian army in the field in 276. However, Pyrrhus, able general though he was, had made himself increasingly unpopular among the Sicilian *poleis* both for his blatant power grabbing and for his cavalier treatment of allies, so much so that he was forced to depart from Sicily. Pyrrhus's fleet suffered a heavy defeat at sea at the hands of the Carthaginian navy, and he would go on to a crippling campaign in southern Italy which eventually resulted in Rome absorbing virtually the entire lower half of the Italian peninsula into its own domains, bringing its borders onto Carthage's Sicilian doorstep. Something had to give.

After a period of increased tension, the inevitable war finally erupted in 264. With the domination of many of the city states, and with only Syracuse the true threat, the Carthaginians decided that they had invested far too much money, time and effort in their war against the Greek city states to simply abandon the field. Carthage, with its eyes firmly resting upon a future ripe with financial possibilities as well as the ability to allow Carthaginian colonization, settled in for the long haul. Shortly after the decision was made to continue the effort, though, the ruler of Syracuse died, and as far as the Carthaginians knew the resistance had ended.

This was not the case. A group of Italian mercenaries who had been hired by the city of Syracuse started to make their way back to Italy when they stopped in the city of Messana, which offered them rest and hospitality before continuing their journey. The mercenaries took advantage of the situation and "treacherously seized Messana…they expelled or slew the male inhabitants, divided their wives and children" (Smith, The Punic Wars, 3) and took control of the city. These mercenaries decided to call themselves "the children of Mamers, or Mars" (Smith, The Punic Wars, 3) and sought to establish themselves as a power. Carthage disagreed with that plan.

When Carthage learned of the treachery of the mercenaries they started to march upon the city of Messana. It was the Carthaginians' intent to punish and capture those mercenaries that they could. The mercenaries, upon discovering that they were now in the path of Carthage's fury, found their courage wanting. The mercenaries decided to "petition Rome to intercede" upon their behalf. The mercenaries reminded the Roman Senate in their plea that the mercenaries were Italians and that it was the responsibility and duty of Rome to come to their aid. To leave the mercenaries to the fate which Carthage was going to dictate would show that Rome had no power over Sicily, and that, more importantly, Rome was ignoring its responsibilities to watch out for its Latin brethren.

For its part, Carthage was not concerned with any plea that the mercenaries made. Carthage believed that the treachery of the mercenaries, so foreign to the rigorous decorum and high moral standards of the Roman culture, would prohibit the Roman Senate from voting to send any sort of assistance to the mercenaries.

However, Rome's reasons for fighting the First Punic War were as clear cut as Carthage's. Rome sought to not only protect its own holdings in Sicily (as well as their allies), they were also concerned about either the Greeks or the Carthaginians increasing their strength on the island. Such a buildup of strength would directly affect the safety of Rome itself.

In addition to protecting itself Rome also had economic reasons. Obtaining more influence on Sicily would increase trade and the ability to export materials to new markets. City states defeated would not only be allied to Rome but some of the conquered states' lands would be doled out to worthy Roman citizens.

Thus, when the Italians who had seized Messana sent a delegation to the Roman Senate seeking assistance, the Roman Senate could not "refuse to protect Italians who appealed to them avowedly as the head of the Italian confederation for aid against the Greeks and Carthaginians" (Smith, The Punic Wars, 5). The Roman Senate, honor bound, could not "look calmly on while the city of Messana fell into the hands of the Carthaginians." (Smith, The Punic Wars, 5).

Understanding these needs, the Roman consuls found that they were able "to raise a patriotic cry of Italians against foreigners." (Smith, The Punic Wars, 6). With this public backing, the Roman government could successfully prepare the state for war against Carthage.

In addition to the requirements of Roman honor, there was the basic necessity to maintain the protective barrier around the city of Rome. The Roman Senate understood that the city of Messana could be used by the Carthaginians "as a standing menace to their [Roman] power and a vantage ground in the great conflict." (Smith, The Punic Wars, 5). The Roman government was quite sure this would be the case was in the near future.

The First Punic War

Rome sought a reason for going to war beyond a simple desire for power, and they found it in the Campanian mercenaries. With the decision made to go to war under the pretense of protecting other Italians, the Romans sent an army to Sicily. This army was commanded by Appius Claudius Caudex and consisted of two legions, close to 10,000 troops. These two ,legions waited in the town of Rhegium on the Italian coast while a Roman tribune by the name of Gaius Claudius slipped across the strait between Sicily and Italy and stole into the city of Messana, where he informed the citizens that Rome was coming to free them from the Carthaginian threat.

While the petitioners from Messana had been in Rome pleading their case, however, Carthage had moved forward with its plan to take complete control of Sicily. The Carthaginians had sent a unit under the command of an officer named Hanno to Messana and seized the city. After Gaius Claudius promised to liberate the citizens from Carthaginian control, Rome launched a small fleet towards Messana, but the Roman ships failed to navigate the currents properly and were forced to return to Rhegium, losing several ships in the process. Some of these ships were captured by the Carthaginian garrison on Messana when they were forced to land.

The Carthaginian commander, Hanno, attempted to avoid a war between Carthage and Rome by sending the ships, crews, and troops back to Rhegium, but Rome was not to be swayed from its intended course of action. Once the fleet reunited, Appius Claudius Caudex crossed the strait once more, and now that the ships' captains were familiar with the currents which ran between Rhegium and Messana, a night crossing was attempted and achieved.

The Roman forces disembarked and formed up so that when the Carthaginian commander looked out in the morning, he saw two full legions were prepared to assault the city. Consul Caudex sent a messenger to the city to request that Hanno meet him in the neutral zone between the Roman army and the city of Messana. Still hoping to prevent outright war between the two powers, Hanno agreed to meet with Caudex, but when Hanno arrived, Caudex had the Carthaginian commander seized. Caudex made sure that Hanno's choice was a simple one: Hanno could surrender the city to the Romans and receive safe passage and his personal liberty, or Hanno would be executed and the city of Messana seized.

Perhaps not surprisingly, Hanno chose his life and liberty over the city. Thus, with his small garrison force, Hanno withdrew from Messana, marching to meet up with other Carthaginian units. Caudex took control of Messana and established positions around the city.

Hanno's absence from the outskirts of Messana was to be short lived, however. Both Carthage and Syracuse were horrified at the entrance of Rome into the fray for Sicily. Carthage's surprise came from the simple fact that they had a treaty of mutual support with Rome, and Rome, having landed in Sicily, should have offered its support to Carthage against the Greek city of Syracuse. Syracuse for its part preferred the devil that it knew to the demon that it didn't. As a result, in a move that surprised the Roman Senate, the city of Syracuse and the Carthaginians set aside their differences and formed an alliance to drive the Roman army off of the island.

Having this goal in mind, the joint Greek and Carthaginian forces marched upon Messana while elements of the formidable Carthaginian navy moved into position to the north to offer support should Roman reinforcements sail for from Rhegium or if the Roman army in Messana attempted flight from the city via the sea. The complementary force from Syracuse was under the command of the Greek Hiero, the king of Syracuse, while the Carthaginian force was under the command of Hanno. Hanno established a camp to the west of Messana, while the Greek forces took up a position to the city's south.

Appius Claudius Caudex, with the self-assuredness of a general in command of two legions of Roman troops, sent out an envoy to the Greeks and Carthaginians with the demand that they abandon their positions. When the Greeks and Carthaginians refused, Caudex promptly declared war upon Carthage, officially starting the First Punic War.

With their refusal hardly having left their lips, Caudex moved against the Greeks and Carthaginians. He first launched an attack upon the Greek forces under the command of Hiero, and the Roman legions quickly drove the Greeks from their camp before pressing on towards the camp of the Carthaginians. They also evicted this force, thereby retaining control of the city of Messana and establishing themselves as a sincere threat to the island's previous status quo.

Hiero fell back immediately to the city of Syracuse and sent out envoys to Caudex. The king of Syracuse sued for peace with Rome and sought an alliance with the Romans, declaring that he would fight against the Carthaginians. Within a year of the battle of Messana an official alliance was struck between Syracuse and Rome and the new allies moved together against the Carthaginian forces.

Hanno, in the meantime, steadily withdrew to the Sicilian city of Acragas, leaving garrisons at various towns. However, the Roman led alliance drove through Sicily, capturing Carthaginian held towns and pushing their forces back. Despite having inferior numbers, the Romans laid siege to the Carthaginian stronghold of Agrigentum for seven months, inflicting thousands of casualties and finally taking the city in 262. This left the Carthaginians with few positions of strength on the island, and it was at this point that the Carthaginian method for the construction of an army first began to fail them.

In the First Punic War, as in previous conflicts, Carthage had relied upon the hiring of mercenary troops. These troops, coming from all around the Mediterranean and specializing in a wide array of weapons and tactics, were commanded by their own native officers. The various mercenary units, however, were under the command of a professional Carthaginian soldier. On Sicily, the Carthaginians had landed their mercenary units, but never together or with a clearly designed or coordinated plan of attack.

The Battle of Agrigentum also caused a shift in policy among the Carthaginian military elite. Rather than face the legions on land, they would attempt to resolve the conflict at sea, where their massive and highly proficient professional navy had the advantage.

That said, with few positions of strength remaining to them on the island, the Carthaginian forces under the command of the Carthaginian Hamilcar Barca opted to attack Italy. By using the Carthaginian navy and its skill upon the seas, Hamilcar launched a series of raids along the Italian coast in an effort to bring the war home to the Romans and to force Rome to withdraw its forces from Sicily. Rome did not withdraw, however, nor did it relinquish any territory which it had gained. Instead, it held firmly onto the conquests they had made on land.

That said, by 260 BCE it was clear that the war's focus would switch to the sea. Indeed, as it would turn out, the "decisive actions in the First Punic War were on the seas." (US Army Command and General Staff College, *Force Projection in the Punic Wars*, 3). For Rome, the First Punic War was the beginning of its martial navy; while Rome had sailors who were fairly adept at plying the trade routes through the Mediterranean, they didn't enjoy any sort of maritime prowess in regards to warfare upon the sea. Upon the outbreak of war with Carthage, however, this all changed. The Carthaginians were the undeniable superpower on the Mediterranean and had been for centuries; they could, quite literally, sail circles around the Roman navy at the beginning of the war. The Romans, however, were quick learners, something the Carthaginians discovered to their detriment, and the First Punic War saw the "largest naval engagements until the 20th century." (US Army Command and General Staff College, *Force Projection in the Punic Wars*, 9).

At the beginning of the war, the Carthaginian navy, manned by native Carthaginians and not mercenaries, were fully capable of defeating the few ships which the Romans were able to launch. The Carthaginian navy was also able to force the Roman troopships off of their marks, making them land farther from their intended destinations or forcing them to attempt night crossings, which were always dangerous even for the most skilled sailors. Rome, however, soon learned how to build ships equal to the Carthaginians' through the capture of the Carthaginian ship.

The Roman navy was dealt a crushing defeat at the Battle of Lipara, but Rome did not take this defeat lying down. Instead, the Senate authorized a massive financial package for the navy, boosting wartime production to hitherto untold (and virtually unsustainable) levels so that more than 100 Roman triremes were constructed within less than two months, a monumental undertaking. Once Rome had the ships, however, the Romans still needed to find experienced captains and crews to use those ships effectively, so a stopgap solution was developed: the *corvus*. Rather than ram the enemy ships and try to sink them, the Roman galleys would close alongside the Carthaginians and then drop the *corvus*, a hook-ended bridge, onto the enemy deck, linking the ships together. Once that was in place, Roman legionaries would swarm across the bridge, effectively turning a naval battle into a land one and returning the combat to terms which were favorable to them. The Carthaginians suffered grievously at the hands of this brilliantly simple device (though it was eventually phased out of service as the Roman navy became as adept as its Punic counterpart) and would gradually lose supremacy on the Mediterranean over the duration of the war.

By 257 BCE, Carthaginians had ceased their raids upon Italy, as Hamilcar Barca had been forced to break off the engagements due to a lack of funds and logistical support from Carthage. A year later, the Romans decided to test their burgeoning naval skills once more in what would be known as the Battle of Cape Ecnomus, perhaps the largest naval battle in all of antiquity. Both fleets were of such immense size that each one had two separate commanders; for the Roman fleet, these commanders were the consuls Marcus Atalius Regulus and Lucius Manlius, while the Carthaginian commanders were Hanno and Hamilcar. Both Hanno and Hamilcar were battle tested commanders, while the consuls were elected officials.

The forces were evenly matched in spite of the Roman navy's relative youth and inexperience, and the battle was a long and fierce fight. Eventually, the Romans defeated the Carthaginians and drove them away from the Italian coast, taking hold of the ships abandoned by the Carthaginians and adding them to their fleet. With their victory at Ecnomus, Rome had successfully driven the war away from Italy and opened the path to North Africa, which would let them bring the war to the Carthaginians.

With the sea lanes to North Africa open, the Romans prepared an invasion force to assault the Carthaginian home territory, and in 255 they landed their legions in North Africa seeking to crush the Carthaginians. Naturally, the Carthaginians did not wait while Rome moved towards Carthage; the city's government sought out a commander for their mercenary army and chose a Spartan trained general, a Greek mercenary by the name of Xanthippos. The Carthaginians, changing their policy of keeping only a Carthaginian in the position of supreme command, hired Xanthippos and brought him to Carthage.

Once in the city, Xanthippos went amongst the mercenaries, some of whom he had fought with and others whom he had fought against. These mercenaries knew the merits and victories of Xanthippos and gave him a measure of respect that no Carthaginian could hope to command, and this respect translated to rapid responses to his orders.

This helped bring about the crucial Carthaginian victory in the battle of Tunis in 255. At that battle, nearly half of the Roman army and the consul Regulus were captured by Xanthippos' troops. The surviving legionaries, about 5,000 men, dug into a position which they could easily defend, and shortly after the battle, the remaining Roman troops were rescued by a portion of the Roman fleet. The Roman defeat at the hands of Xanthippos marked the end of Roman efforts in North Africa.

By 254, the Carthaginian army returned to Sicily in an effort to take back their lost holdings and to seize the entire island. At the same time, Carthage made the decision to release Xanthippos, so in 251, Hasdrubal was the commander of the Carthaginian forces on Sicily. In the northwest of Sicily, the Roman and Carthaginian forces met in the battle of Panormus, and Hasdrubal's troops were defeated and pushed back, eliciting an attempt at peace negotiations from the Carthaginians. This gesture was made through the release of the consul Regulus who had been captured at the battle of Tunis.

A bust of Hasdrubal

Carthage sought a prisoner exchange if peace was not preferred, but ironically, Regulus advised against peace and against the prisoner exchange, convincing the Roman Senate that the continuation of the war was necessary. In the honorable Roman norm, Regulus returned to Carthage where he delivered the Senate's refusal to both peace and an exchange of prisoners. The Carthaginians, in turn, tortured him to death for failing to secure even a prisoner exchange.

As the war continued, the next major battle between the two opponents occurred off of the coast of Sicily at the battle of Drepanum. This battle took place in 249 between a Carthaginian fleet commanded by Admiral Adherbal and a Roman fleet commanded by the consul Publius Claudius Pulcher, while on land, the Romans laid siege to the Carthaginian controlled cities of Drepanum and Lilybaeum.

When the two fleets met upon the seas, Pulcher's lack of significant military experience led to a resounding defeat for the Romans. In fact, the loss of Roman ships was so severe that it took the Romans nearly a decade to rebuild their fleet. On land, the Romans could no longer successfully continue their sieges and were forced almost into guerrilla warfare, with the commanders focused on repelling Carthaginian landings on Sicily.

In 247, the Carthaginians succeeded in landing the general Hamilcar Barca upon Sicily. Though ill-supplied and with few replacements, Barca successfully kept the Romans from taking the islands. By 242, however, he was no longer able to hold the Romans back, and the Roman legions took the Carthaginian held cities of Lilybaeum and Drepanum.

In 241, Carthage launched a fleet under the command of another admiral named Hanno in an effort to resupply Barca and once more secure Carthaginian positions on Sicily, but a Roman fleet under the command of consul Lutatius Catulus sailed out to intercept the Carthaginians. Over the previous twenty three years of war Rome had learned to master the sea. With this knowledge – and with their ships prepared for war – they met the supply laden Carthaginian ships, and the defeat suffered by the Carthaginians was so devastating that it convinced them to sue for peace.

With general Hamilcar Barca given the power to treat for peace, he met with consul Catulus. Catulus offered generous terms which Barca readily accepted. Both sides agreed to not continue any hostilities towards the enemy's allies. Carthage, however, would be forced to abandon all of their holdings on Sicily. In addition to this, no Punic ships of war could enter Italian waters, the Carthaginians would be forced to pay a heavy restitution, and they had to release 8,000 Roman prisoners. All of these blows badly crippled the Carthaginian economy.

The end of the First Punic War brought a decisive shift of power in the Mediterranean. Prior to the outbreak of the war, Carthage was the reigning power, dominating the shipping lanes, ports, and trade. They controlled allies and territories with mercenary troops and gained allies and territories in the same fashion. Rome, while a strong power, was not considered the equal to Carthage, but after 23 years of war, the Romans were victorious. The terms of peace dealt serious blows to the Carthaginian economy, and the humiliation helped ensure there would be a

Second Punic War several decades later.

The result of the First Punic War was a complete dearth of cash in Carthage, which was a serious problem because Carthage relied chiefly on mercenary armies. Thousands of mercenaries throughout the Carthaginian Empire were suddenly not getting their wages, and the result was inevitable: war. An all-out insurrection of mercenary contingents throughout the Punic Empire, including Iberia, Sardinia and Corsica, and a renewed attack from the subjugated Lybian tribes, followed. Suddenly, Carthage was fighting for her very life, and grudgingly accepting military and financial aid from her two old enemies, Syracuse and Rome.

The war dragged on for two years, but by 238 Carthage was once again secure, with order restored to her dominions. Still, the cost had been heavy; taking advantage of Carthage's desperate situation, Rome had conveniently seized both Sardinia and Corsica, which had been plunged into lawlessness by the mercenary uprising, and there was nothing Carthage could do about it. The mines of Iberia, with their vast amounts of as yet untapped wealth, were still secure, but control of them was dubious.

The Roman victory over Carthage in the First Punic War made a second war all but inevitable, but had Rome lost the First Punic War, the consequences may not have been quite as dire as might be imagined. Rome was somewhat unique in the Mediterranean world for its focus on complete and utter subjugation of any enemies, whereas most nations were content with a demonstrable victory in arms, and then an armistice. Part of the reason that the First Punic War dragged on as long as it did was that Rome insisted on so humiliating a victory. Carthage sued for peace several times and was rejected, and when the Romans offered terms, they were so harsh that Carthage could not accept them. The war only ended because both sides were financially and morally exhausted after years of warfare and a small fortune poured into ships and armies. Had Carthage defeated Rome in the First Punic War, Rome may not have reached the heights of influence that it enjoyed among other states in the Mediterranean, and the position of entertaining envoys and pleas for support and friendship. However, Carthage would have been unlikely to seek the total destruction of the Roman Republic as a whole.

Of course, that would change during the Second Punic War.

An Early End to the Second Punic War?

Crisis, as so often occurs, had brought political change in its wake, and the Barcid family, led by Hamilcar Barca, had risen to prominence during the Mercenary Wars. Hamilcar was a skilled general who rapidly rose to command all of the Carthaginian armies by ousting the competition of his rival, Hanno the Great. Hamilcar was populist and had the support of the common people, whereas Hanno was a scion of the old Carthaginian aristocracy, but their power was on the wane. Thus, it was Hamilcar and his son-in-law, Hasdrubal the Fair, who subdued the Iberian cities, but the loyalty of these new dominions was far from certain. Rather than owing allegiance to

Carthage, the Iberian cities looked to Hamilcar exclusively for guidance, making Spain a virtual Barcid fief.

Hamilcar was killed in battle in 228, so Hasdrubal took over as his successor and began to look for a way to strike back at Rome in retaliation for the First Punic War and the blatant land grab in the chaos that followed. It appears likely that around 225, Hasdrubal began plotting with the Gauls of the Po Valley in the north of Italy (the only as yet unconquered area in the Italian Peninsula) to launch an attack on Rome with Carthaginian backing, but the Senate got wind of the plan and ordered a pre-emptive strike of their own, leading to a five-year war which eventually led to the annexation of the Po Valley. Hasdrubal himself was assassinated in 221, possibly with Roman collusion.

Rather than solve the Romans' problem, Hasdrubal's death brought about the rise of the most famous Carthaginian of all. Hasdrubal was succeeded by his brother-in-law and Hamilcar's son, Hannibal. In the history of war, only a select few men always make the list of greatest generals, and one of them is Hannibal, who has the distinction of being the only man who nearly brought Rome to its knees before its decline almost 700 years after his time.

For two years, Hannibal bided his time, consolidating his position in the Iberian peninsula and massing his forces, abiding by one of the greatest military truths and one which doubtless his tutors and his father, with their tales of Alexander and Alcibiades, had contributed to instill in him: numbers do not matter so much as concentration of force, i.e. what troops are available to fight in one single critical location, at any given time. Meanwhile, even as Hannibal was preparing to strike out against their very heart, the Romans seem to have grown unusually complacent; after all, Hannibal was new to overall command, and with both Hamilcar and Hasdrubal dead, they must have felt themselves secure. When in 218 Hannibal resurrected his brother-in-law's plan for a joint Gaulish and Carthaginian invasion of the Italian peninsula, the Romans were caught napping, something which they would live to regret in the following years.

Hannibal needed a *casus belli*, and in 219 BCE the Romans obliged him with one, forming an alliance with the powerful Iberian city of Saguntum, well south of the line drawn along the Ebro, and unilaterally declaring it a Roman protectorate. Hannibal took this for outright rebellion, and acted accordingly, investing the city and besieging it for eight months until it fell. He then protested to Carthage that Rome had broken the terms of their agreement with them, declaring that there could be only one feasible course of action: war. The Carthaginian rulers, having been burned once before, were wary of becoming embroiled in a new conflict with Rome, but such was Hannibal's popularity with the troops in the Iberian peninsula that, with the memory of the Mercenary Wars still fresh in their minds, they acceded to his demands rather than risk a full-blown mutiny.

The siege of Saguntum would last eight months, and seven months in, Saguntum managed to get envoys to Rome to plead for assistance, but whether caught up dealing with rebellions in

Illyria or deliberately delaying to justify their cause of war, Rome did not send any legions in time to save the city. As Saguntum's defenses crumbled, attempts were made to negotiate a peace, with the Carthaginians demanding that the citizens of Saguntum surrender the city in its entirety and leave with only one garment each. They refused. The leading citizens threw their valuables into a fire and many threw themselves on the flames after. The city fell soon after this, and most of the inhabitants either slaughtered or enslaved, with Hannibal collecting a good amount of spoils with which to fund his intended conquest of Rome, and subsequently, the Mediterranean.

Interestingly enough, an event occurred during the siege of Saguntum that almost changed the course of history and would likely have prematurely ended one of the deadliest wars of antiquity before it began. Hannibal led his soldiers with great energy, taking personal part in the siege, operating rams, moving siege engines, and exposing himself to danger along with it. At one point in the battle, he took a very serious javelin wound to the leg. It was enough to take him off the field and halt the active siege for several days, so it must have been quite severe. Had Hannibal been killed so early in the siege of Saguntum, it is likely that the Second Punic War never would have happened. The dream of conquest in Italy was one mostly dear to Hannibal himself, and as events would demonstrate, the Carthaginian Senate never fully committed their support to his operations, even as he subsequently threatened Rome itself. They eventually recalled him to defend in Africa, much to his chagrin.

Without Hannibal at the head of the operation, would any other general have stepped into his place to lead the campaign forward? Would any have had the ambition to take their soldiers over the Alps and threaten the city of Rome itself? As it turned out, Hannibal did survive, took Saguntum, and settled into the city of New Carthage as his base of operations as Rome rallied together legions and commanders and sent a force to Spain to confront the Carthaginians. With that, the Second Punic War had officially begun.

Initially, the war did not go well for Carthage. Hannibal was joined by generals Hasdrubal, Hanno, and Matho, while Roman forces arrived at their allied city of Massalia under the command of the brothers Gnaeus Cornelius Scipio and Publius Cornelius Scipio. Another opportunity for an early end to the war presented itself. Gnaeus Scipio managed two solid defeats of Carthaginian forces quite quickly into the confrontation. He first defeated Hanno at the Battle of Cissa after the Carthaginian made an ill-conceived attack on the Roman forces without waiting for reinforcements under Hasdrubal. Next Hasdrubal attempted a naval attack at the Battle of Ebro River, only to be soundly beaten by the Roman fleet. However, Hannibal and his forces evaded the Roman legions, pushing north of the Ebro, conquering the surrounding Celtiberian tribes, and heading toward the Alps with his eyes on Italy.

If any of the Roman forces could have intercepted Hannibal and brought him to battle there in the Iberian Peninsula, the course of the war would have changed dramatically. Without the pressure of attack on the Italian homeland, the entirety of Roman forces could have been concentrated on the Carthaginians in Spain, and they likely would have emerged victorious. Such an early victory would have saved numerous lives, possibly including those of the Scipio brothers. At the same time, it would have meant that Scipio Africanus would never have risen to the command of the army and made his long-lasting friendship with the Numidians or pursued his own invasion of Africa.

Carthage might have fared better from an early defeat as well. Hannibal's deep hatred of the Romans and calculated attack on Italy itself created a much more personal war for the Romans, and it later compelled Scipio to mount the offensive in Africa in order to draw Hannibal back home out of Italy and mitigate the threat to Rome. Without Hannibal's move against Italy, the countryside of Africa could have remained free of warfare and devastation, the Romans might not have sought such a complete and utter subjugation of Carthage, and Carthage have been able to recover some of its former power and made yet another determined attack on Rome or indeed the surrounding Mediterranean, remaining a powerful player in the centuries to come instead of a shell of its former might.

The Alps

In the spring of 218 BCE, at the head of approximately 50,000 infantry, 15,000 cavalry, and 50 war elephants, Hannibal began marching northeast. His plan was breathtakingly ambitious: he would march through the Pyrenees, across southern Gaul, over the Alps and into Italy proper, thereby avoiding the heavily fortified border in the northwest of Italy. It was a route no general had ever taken before, let alone a general with so many animals (including elephants). His father Hamilcar had been defeated trying to invade southern Italy and attempting to outfight the Roman navy at sea; Hannibal would not make the same mistake.

Pushing aside with contemptuous ease the stiff resistance of the Pyrenean tribes, who contested every step of the way from their strongholds of the mountain passes, Hannibal pushed forwards with remarkable speed, leaving behind a detachment of some 10,000 Iberian soldiers to keep his lines of communication open and pacify the tumultuous region. He then marched on into southern Gaul, negotiating with the local chieftains and outfighting those who had a mind to contest his advance. His speed of maneuver, and his ability to move his army across rough terrain, proved unmatched in the ancient world since the time of Alexander the Great. By that point, his army, which now numbered some 40,000 infantry, 8,000 cavalry, and around 40 war elephants, danced up the valley of the Rhone to evade a Roman force sent to bar his passage southwards through the strategically vital gap in the mountains where the Alps meet the Mediterranean. With that route closed to him, Hannibal, undaunted, struck south and east across the Alps themselves.

Exactly what route he took is still the subject of hotly contested debate today, and even Roman scholars writing shortly after his prodigious feat seem to have no clear idea of where precisely he made his passage, but one thing is certain: it was one of the most remarkable maneuvers in military history. There were no roads greater than a goat-track across the Alps, none of them continuous, and the high passes were smothered by snow, often year-round, with drifts dozens of feet deep. Moreover, those passes included other hazards, such as potential rockfalls, and the barren terrain offered limited supplies. To top it all off, these passes were crawling with bellicose tribesmen who lived by banditry and hid in impregnable fortresses perched atop sheer crags. To Hannibal's army, most of them Iberians from the sun-baked plains of southern Spain or Carthaginians from the hot deserts of Northern Africa, the Alps must have looked like an icy Hell.

Hannibal's passage of the Alps remains the most famous event of his life and legend, and even though the location of his crossing matters little compared to the fact that he ultimately did get across, it has nonetheless been the most compelling mystery of his life for over 2,000 years. Even ancient historians were intrigued and tried to figure out the answer. The well known ancient Greek historian Polybius mentioned that Hannibal's men came into conflict with a Celtic tribe, the Allobroges, which was situated near the northern part of the range along the banks of the river Isère. The famous Roman historian Livy, writing over 150 years after Polybius, claimed Hannibal took a southerly route.

It is believed that both historians used the same source, a soldier in Hannibal's army, Sosylus of Lacedaemon, who wrote a history of the Second Punic War. Geographers and historians have pointed to the 6 most likely mountain passes that could have actually been used and then tried to narrow it down by finding one that seems to match the descriptions of both Livy and Polybius. A handful of historians used those accounts to theorize that Hannibal crossed the Alps at the Col du Montgenèvre pass, which would have been in the southern part of the range near northwest Italy. That also happened to be one of the better known road passes in the ancient world, and it was used often for diplomacy.

Wherever the crossing, and despite the innumerable difficulties, Hannibal got across. He reached the rolling foothills of Northern Italy several months later, at the head of 20,000 infantry, 4,000 cavalry, and a mere handful of war elephants (the great beasts having fared none too well, as was to be expected, in the mountain passes). If figures relating to his troop numbers before and after his celebrated crossing are to be believed, only half of the men Hannibal marched into the Alps marched back out again, and Hannibal must have known that no supply convoys could ever hope to cross where his army had passed. Nor, with the Roman navy's supremacy in the Mediterranean, could he have much hope of resupply or retreat by sea. Like Caesar would do nearly 170 years later crossing the Rubicon, Hannibal had cast the die. He and his men were left with no choice but victory or death.

Depiction of Hannibal's men crossing the Alps

Costly as it was, Hannibal's choice to cross the Alps was not done so for vainglorious reasons. By appearing suddenly in Northern Italy, crossing terrain that was reckoned to be impassable, Hannibal took the Romans completely by surprise, and the main Roman army that had been mobilized to fight Hannibal was caught completely wrong-footed. When news of Hannibal's appearance reached its commander, Publius Scipio (father of the redoubtable Scipio Africanus, who would cross swords with Hannibal himself in the years to come), he was in the process of pushing his men across the Pyrenees and into Iberia. He quickly loaded his rearguard onto ships, sailed across to Italy, and hurried to intercept Hannibal by forced march.

Scipio engaged Hannibal's forces at Ticinus, but he could only hope to fight a delaying action with the limited troops at his disposal. Hannibal's celebrated Numidian cavalry routed Scipio's forces, and would have killed Scipio himself had it not been for Scipio Africanus' timely rescue. Emboldened by this Roman defeat, the Gauls of the Po valley rose in revolt, sending a large force (around 20,000 men) to join Hannibal's army. Hannibal then marched his force south of Scipio's main base at Placentia, on the Trebia river, cutting him off from the support of Consul Sempronius Longus, who was marching up from southern Italy to come to his aid and bring Hannibal to battle. However, when the provisions promised to his army by the Cisalpine Gauls failed to materialize, Hannibal was forced to abandon his tactically superior position to capture the supply depots at Clastidium, allowing Longus and Scipio to join their forces near the Trebia.

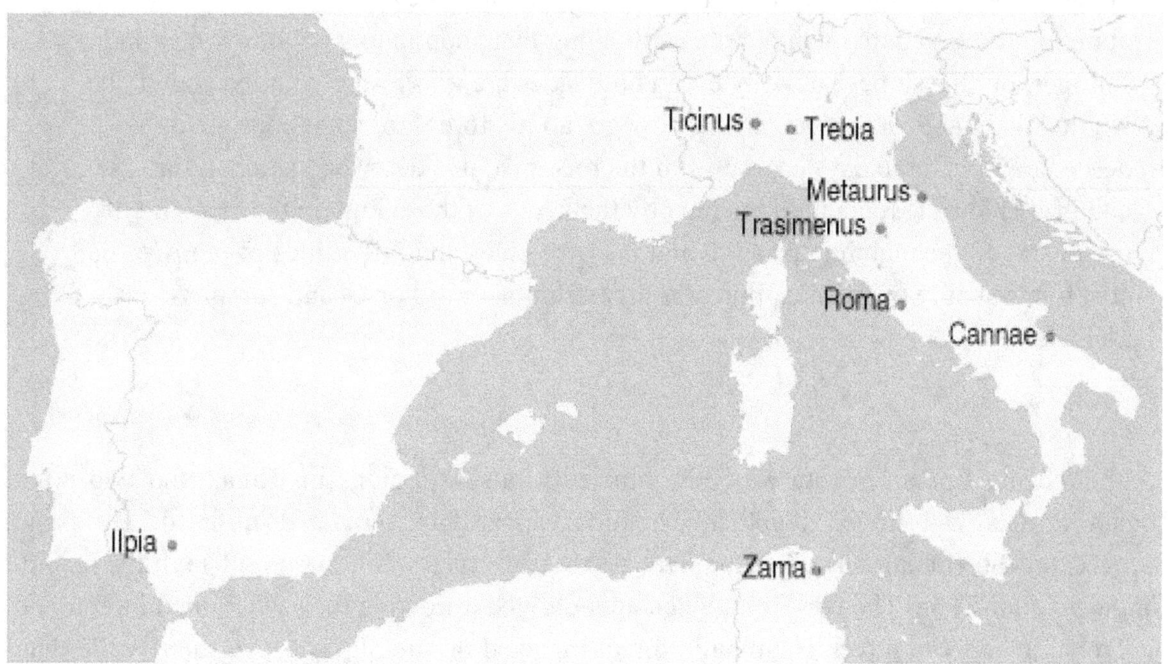

Given the logistical difficulties, it was not a given that Hannibal and the Carthaginians would survive the march. The ancient historian Polybius described what the Carthaginians had to go through just to make it to Italy:

"During this he encountered no enemy, except a few skulking marauders, but owing to the difficulties of the ground and the snow his losses were nearly as heavy as on the ascent. The descending path was very narrow and steep, and as both men and beasts could not tell on what they were treading owing to the snow, all that stepped wide of the path or stumbled were dashed down the precipice. This trial, however, they put up with, being by this time familiar with such sufferings, but they at length reached a place where it was impossible for either the elephants or the pack-animals to pass owing to the extreme narrowness of the path, a previous landslip having carried away…and here the soldiers once more became disheartened and discouraged. The Carthaginian general at first thought of avoiding the difficult part by a detour, but as a fresh fall of snow made progress impossible he had to abandon this project…As for the men, when, unable to pierce the lower layer of snow, they fell and then tried to help themselves to rise by the support of their knees and hands, they slid along still more rapidly on these, the slope being exceedingly steep. But the animals, when they fell, broke through the lower layer of snow in their efforts to rise, and remained there with their packs as if frozen into it, owing to their weight and the congealed condition of this old snow. Giving up this project, then, Hannibal encamped on the ridge, sweeping it clear of snow, and next set the soldiers to work to build up the path along the cliff, a most toilsome task…with great difficulty in three days he managed to get the elephants across, but in a wretched condition from hunger; for the summits of the Alps and the parts near the tops of the passes are all quite treeless and bare owing to the snow lying there continuously both winter and summer, but the slopes half-way up on both sides are grassy and wooded and on the whole inhabitable. Hannibal having now got all his forces together continued the descent, and in three days' march from the precipice just described reached flat country. He had lost many of his men by the hands of the enemy in the crossing of rivers and on the march in general, and the precipices and difficulties of the Alps had cost him not only many men, but a far greater number of horses and sumpter-animals."[1]

Fighting in Italy

Although the Roman Senate was now hurriedly raising legions in Rome, and two powerful Roman armies had joined together, Hannibal apparently remained unfazed. He promptly marched on the Roman camp on the Trebia, making a show of force and inviting Scipio and Longus to attack him. The two Roman generals obliged, throwing their celebrated infantry across the Trebia in order to attack Hannibal's forces, arrayed on the bluffs above the river. Exhausted by their river crossing, the Roman troops became entangled in a bloody melee with Hannibal's infantry, fighting each other to a standstill until Hannibal unveiled his master stroke. Concealed from the Roman infantry by the terrain until the last moment, his light infantry and cavalry stormed into the Roman flanks, enveloped the entire force and, trapping the legions with their backs to the river, annihilated them. It was a crushing victory for Hannibal, and a disaster for Rome. It would be the first of many.

---

[1] Polybius, 3.54.3-3.56.2

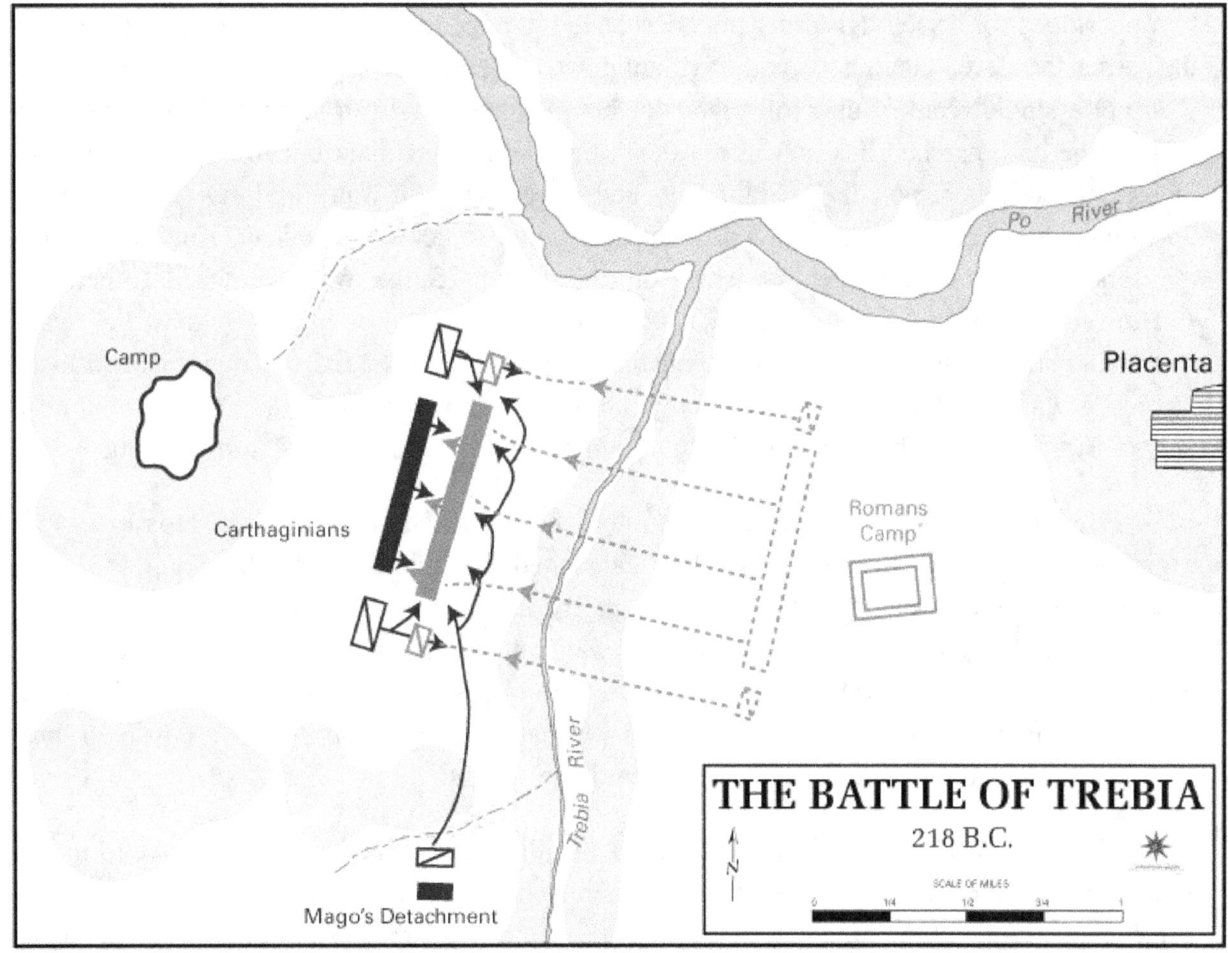

By this point, the campaigning season, which traditionally stopped during the winter months, was virtually over. Hannibal decided to winter his troops in Cisalpine Gaul, but he quickly wore out his welcome there. Possibly because the Gauls were displeased at how Hannibal had used their levies to grind down the Roman forces, the supplies they provided were stilted and ungenerous. In early spring, Hannibal decided to find himself a more secure base and made ready to carry the war into Italy proper. However, despite the winter lull, the Romans had not been idle. Two consular armies, under consuls Servilius and Flaminius, had marched at the beginning of the new year to block Hannibal's routes to the south and east, fortifying their positions there and effectively immuring him within northern Italy. A normal general would have thought himself trapped. Hannibal, however, had a plan. To the south lay the Apennines Mountains and the huge swampy delta of the Arno river, in modern Tuscany, an area reckoned impassable by any army.

Hannibal must have reckoned that after what he had faced in the Alps, he and his men were ready for any challenge. After a brief pause for consideration, he ordered his army to march for the Arno. The Apennines were less of a challenge than the Alps had been, and Hannibal's forces made decent enough time as they crossed through them, but Hannibal himself suffered a debilitating injury, losing an eye to a virulent infection (believed to be conjunctivitis) that kept him bedridden for a spell. His army then descended into the basin of the Arno, but the going was far harder than even Hannibal could have anticipated. The entire region was a festering swamp, with not a single scrap of dry, solid land for his men and horses to sleep on. Hannibal quickly realized he had marched his men into a death-trap. With no choice but to push on, he and his men marched uninterruptedly for four days and three nights, in water and mud that often came up to their waists, with no rest except what they could snatch on their feet. Hundreds, perhaps thousands of Hannibal's men perished on the march. Some were drowned, others were swallowed by quicksand, others contracted malaria or dysentery from drinking the swampy water, and still more simply died of exhaustion. By the end of the march, Hannibal had lost the last of his war elephants, as well as virtually all of his supplies and wheeled transport, but he was now in Etruria, Roman heartland, with both Flaminius and Servilius to the north of him.

As Polybius noted in his account, Hannibal had reached an important crossroad in his campaign. As Polybius wrote, "[Hannibal] calculated that, if he passed the camp and made a descent into the district beyond, Flaminius (partly for fear of popular reproach and partly of personal irritation) would be unable to endure watching passively the devastation of the country but would spontaneously follow him…and give him opportunities for attack." Hannibal needed to bring Flaminius to battle, to avoid the danger of having a large enemy force to his rear, but he found Flaminius too passive to give him the battle he sought.

In order to persuade the Consul – who had a healthy fear of his abilities – to take to the field against him, Hannibal set about ravaging the surrounding Etrurian countryside, sacking towns, burning markets and generally wreaking havoc in the hope that Flaminius would become so incensed that he would be forced to defend the Italian heartland, or that a direct order should arrive from Rome ordering him to do so. Hannibal, though his military strategy was sound, was not as strong in his political choices as he was in battle: by devastating Etruria, he lost support among the local people, whom he might otherwise have been able to lure away from their alliance to Rome. Moreover, despite Hannibal's best efforts, Flaminius stubbornly stayed put in his defensive position. Frustrated by the Roman general's supineness, Hannibal marched around Flaminius's flank and cut him off from Rome, the kind of turning movement in warfare that was rarely used in the ancient world but became standard fare (and often the ultimate strategic goal) over the next 2,000 years. Even with such a massive threat to his lines of supply and communication, Flaminius still refused to march, so Hannibal turned and marched southwards. This time, with the Senate demanding what exactly he was playing at, Flaminius had no choice but to chase him.

Flaminius marched his 30,000 men after Hannibal, but the Carthaginian forces outstripped him. Desperate to bring the enemy to battle, Flaminius pushed recklessly onwards without scouting his line of advance, a mistake which was to cost him dear. On the northern edge of Lake Trasimene, Flaminius marched his army through a narrow defile and onto a small plain that was ringed by wooded mountains, through which his trackers reported Hannibal had marched some time previously. It was only when the last of the Roman forces had marched through the defile that Hannibal swung the jaws of his trap shut: his cavalry rushed forward from concealed positions to close the only gap through which Flaminius's force could retreat, and then his entire army poured howling out of the woods and fell onto the Romans before they had the chance to take up battle positions. In the ensuing desperate melee, virtually the entire Roman army was wiped out: 15,000 or more, including Flaminius himself, were killed, cut down in the melee or drowned in the lake trying to swim to safety. Around 5,000 more Roman soldiers were captured, and the remainder scattered into the hills. In one masterful stroke, Hannibal had disposed of the last field army in Northern Italy, successfully executing antiquity's greatest ambush. Rome herself was now at his mercy.

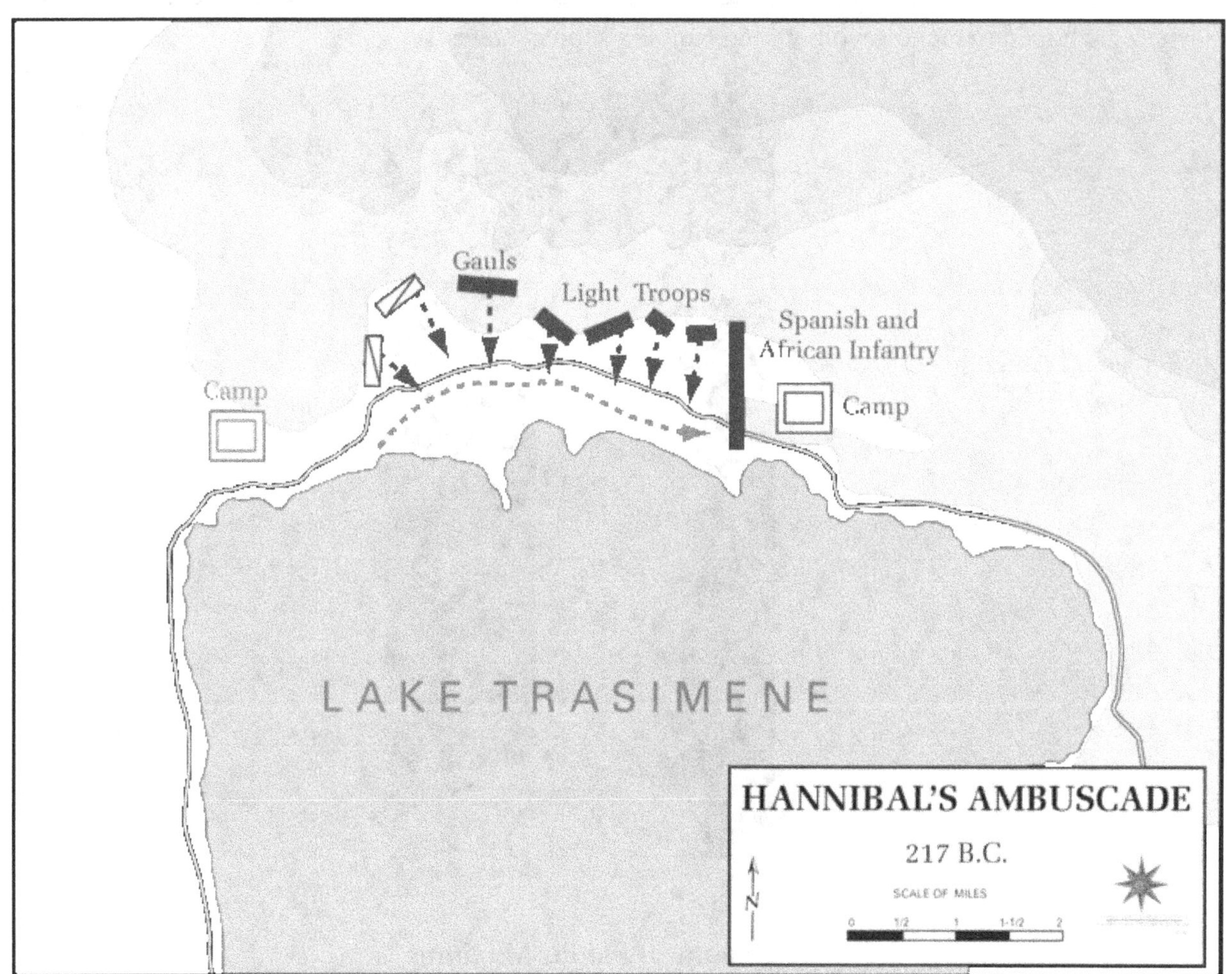

According to the ancient Roman writer Livy, "Such was the uproar and confusion that neither counsel nor command could be heard, and so far was the soldier from recognising his standard or his company or his place in the rank, that he had hardly sufficient presence of mind to get hold of his weapons and make them available for use, and some who found them a burden rather than a protection were overtaken by the enemy. In such a thick fog ears were of more use than eyes; the men turned their gaze in every direction as they heard the groans of the wounded and the blows on shield or breastplate, and the mingled shouts of triumph and cries of panic. Some who tried to fly ran into a dense body of combatants and could get no further; others who were returning to the fray were swept away by a rush of fugitives."[2]

Hannibal was now in an ideal position to strike at Rome, but he chose not to do so. If he ever had any siege artillery in his baggage train (no mention is made of it in the original sources) then he lost it in the Alps or in the swamps of the Arno, because he had none available to invest Rome, nor, apparently, the engineering expertise either among his Carthaginian troops or his Gaulish levies to manufacture any. Without siege engines, he could still have chosen to ring the city with earthworks and lay siege to it, but instead he decided to march into Southern Italy, where he hoped to incite revolt among Rome's subject states.

Statue of Fabius Maximus

The Romans, desperate for something, anything, to rid themselves of this Carthaginian Nemesis, appointed General Fabius Maximus as Dictator, an extraordinary measure which was only undertaken in times of the greatest crisis. Maximus, who had a healthy respect for Hannibal's generalship and was painfully aware of what had befallen Roman armies in pitched battles against him, now developed the "Fabian Strategy", which focused on indirect, attritional

---

[2] Livy, 22.5

warfare. This strategy called for relying on skirmishes, ambushes, and dilatory tactics to harass, undermine and frighten Hannibal's forces, avoiding pitched battle which would almost certainly have proven ruinous. Though Maximus' tactics were effective, this indirect mode of warfare was considered dishonorable, even cowardly, by many Romans, who derisively nicknamed him "Cunctator" ("The Delayer").

Frustrated by Maximus' tactics, Hannibal took out his spite by ravaging the country estates and cities of the Apulian region before making his way into Campania, one of the most important agrarian regions in Italy because of its vast fertile plains that produced harvests crucial to feeding the great masses of Rome. Even the threat to the Campanian exports failed to draw Maximus into open battle, but Hannibal was so overzealous in his harrowing of Campania that, he soon realized, come the winter his army would have nothing to live off. Accordingly, he decided to march back to Apulia, but found his path blocked by a number of different Roman contingents that Maximus had placed at crucial passes to bar his way back. Hannibal responded with customary brilliance, by feinting his entire army at a thickly wooded hill, suggesting he was going to march through the forest and ignore the pass, and when the Roman army repositioned to attempt to bar his way, promptly marched his men about and through the pass they had so obligingly left unguarded, a tactical master-stroke which so damaged Maximus' already tarnished reputation as a commander that he was forced to step down as Dictator. As British historian Adrian Goldsworthy noted, the maneuver was "a classic of ancient generalship, finding its way into nearly every historical narrative of the war and being used by later military manuals".

Hannibal spent the winter comfortably ensconced in Apulia, raiding the region to procure supplies for his army and making overtures to the Macedonians, the city-states of Syracuse, and many other erstwhile allies of Rome. He needed their help in the hopes they would provide him with men and supplies which were desperately needed since Carthage stubbornly refused to support him. Despite his successes, Hannibal was not particularly politically beloved at home, with many believing he was being too rash in provoking Rome. Frustrated, Hannibal resumed the campaigning season in the spring of 216 BCE by capturing the city of Cannae, a crucial supply hub, and placing himself along the line that convoys from the ports and warehouses of the south needed to travel to reach Rome. This was something the Romans could not and did not take lying down. Rome raised the largest army in their city's history, a force of between 80,000 and 100,000 men, and marched south with Consuls Varro and Paullus at the head of the army. This military behemoth disregarded the delaying tactics that Maximus had favored, fully determined to destroy Hannibal once and for all as quickly as possible. Polybius described the unprecedented nature of this Roman army: "The Senate determined to bring eight legions into the field, which had never been done at Rome before, each legion consisting of five thousand men besides allies. ...Most of their wars are decided by one consul and two legions, with their quota of allies; and they rarely employ all four at one time and on one service. But on this occasion, so great was the alarm and terror of what would happen, they resolved to bring not only four but eight legions into the field."

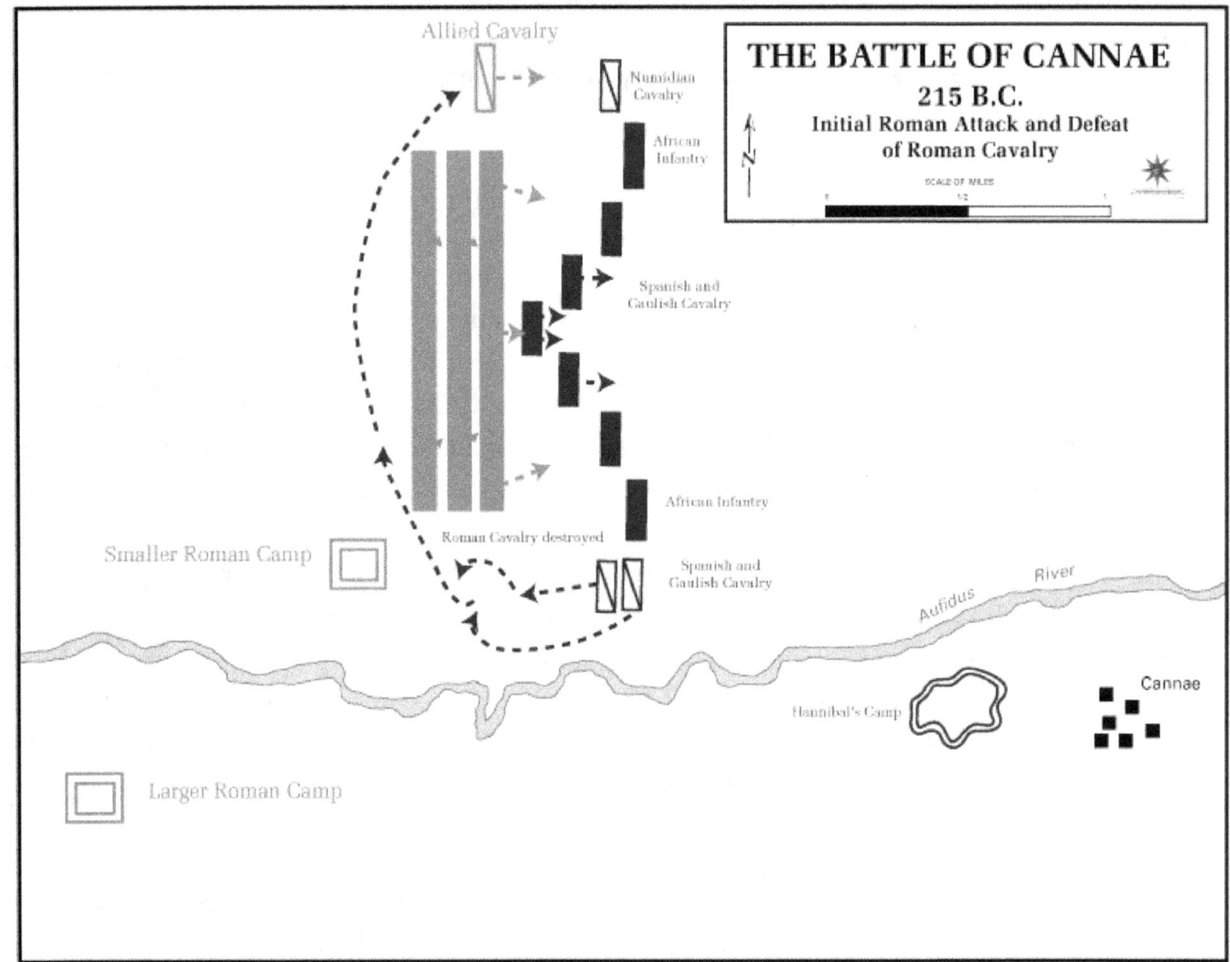

The lines at the beginning of the battle

Despite the massive horde headed his way, Hannibal was ready for them. He encamped his army near the Aufidus, a river not far from Cannae, and waited. His intelligence told him that Consul Varro, the more influential of the two Roman generals, was a firebrand, talented in attack but with a tendency to overreach himself, and Hannibal resolved to use this flaw to his advantage. Hannibal arrayed his army in the open, sure that Varro would be unable to resist the temptation to offer battle, and then deliberately placed his weakest infantry in the center of his battle-line. Varro led the Roman legions straight at the centre of Hannibal's formation, proceeding in characteristic bull-headed fashion and spearheading the assault himself. Hannibal's troops in the center yielded before the legions, as Hannibal had anticipated, sucking the bulk of the Roman force deep into the centre of Hannibal's formation. Meanwhile, the wings of Hannibal's infantry automatically swung against the flanks of the Roman force while Hannibal's cavalry, led by his celebrated general Maharbal, crushed the Roman cavalry and light infantry deployed to protect the formation's flanks and rear and, in so doing, succeeded   in encircling it completely. The Roman force now found itself unable to run or maneuver, completely surrounded by Hannibal's forces. It was one of the earliest examples of the pincer movement in the history of warfare.

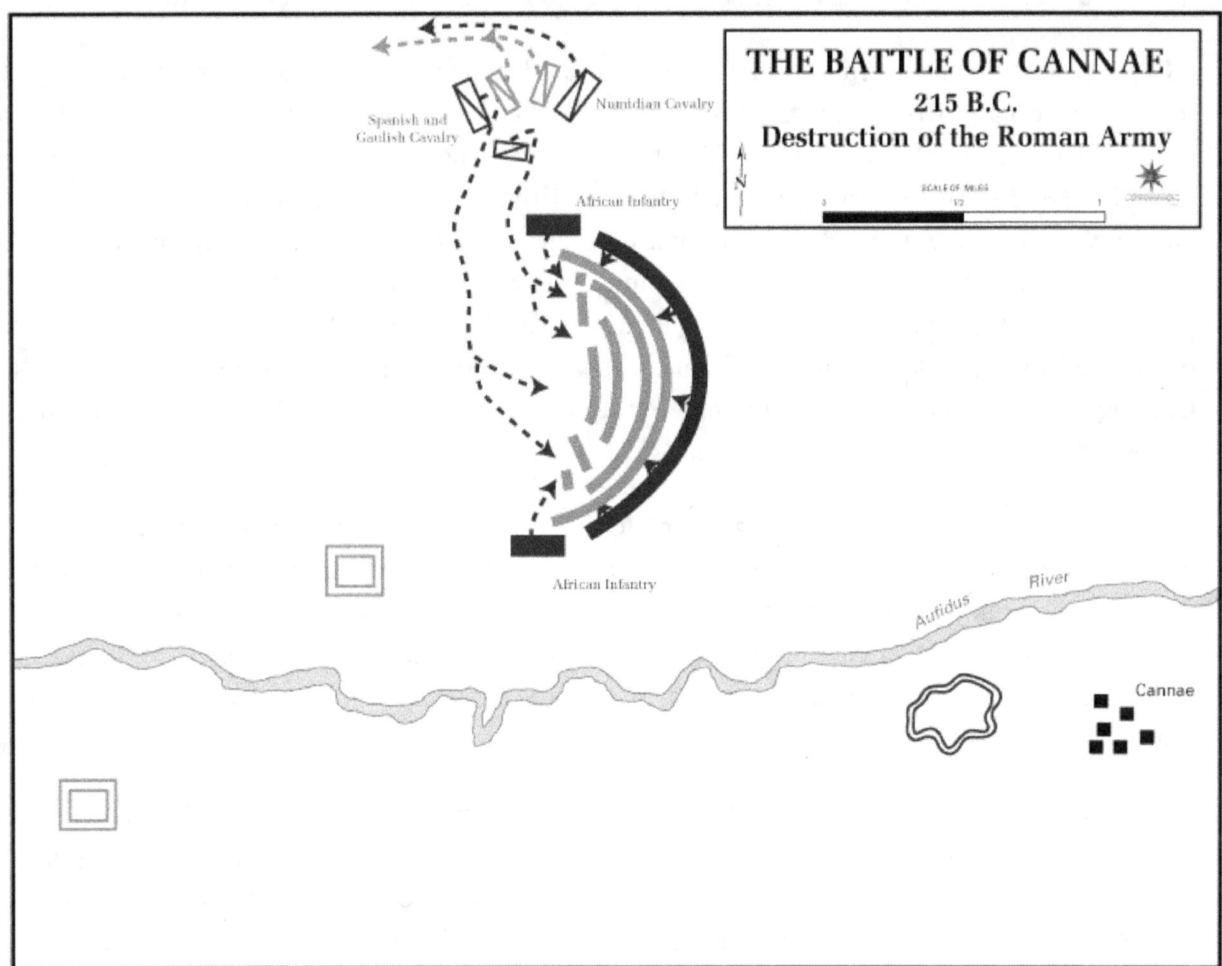

It was a massacre, one of the most vicious battles in the history of the world. Around 75% of the Roman army was cut down in the ensuing melee, which would be in the vicinity of between 50,000-80,000 soldiers depending on which initial estimates are considered to be accurate. Among the casualties was the luckless Consul Paullus, two-thirds of the city's Military Tribunes, a host of officials and noblemen from the most prominent Roman families, and almost a full third of the Senate. Hannibal's army killed so many prominent Romans that his men collected more than 200 gold signets from dead Romans, and he had the rings sent to Carthage to demonstrate his complete victory.

Livy described the scene, "So many thousands of Romans were dying ... Some, whom their wounds, pinched by the morning cold, had roused, as they were rising up, covered with blood, from the midst of the heaps of slain, were overpowered by the enemy. Some were found with their heads plunged into the earth, which they had excavated; having thus, as it appeared, made pits for themselves, and having suffocated themselves." If the casualty numbers are accurate, Hannibal's army slaughtered an average of 600 Roman soldiers every minute until nightfall ended the battle, and less than 15,000 Roman troops escaped, which required cutting their way through the center of Hannibal's army and fleeing to the nearby town of Canusium.

Cannae is still considered one of the greatest tactical victories in the history of warfare. As military historian Theodore Dodge described, "Few battles of ancient times are more marked by ability...than the battle of Cannae. The position was such as to place every advantage on Hannibal's side. The manner in which the far from perfect Hispanic and Gallic foot was advanced in a wedge in échelon... was first held there and then withdrawn step by step, until it had reached the converse position... is a simple masterpiece of battle tactics. The advance at the proper moment of the African infantry, and its wheel right and left upon the flanks of the disordered and crowded Roman legionaries, is far beyond praise. The whole battle, from the Carthaginian standpoint, is a consummate piece of art, having no superior, few equal, examples in the history of war."

Furthermore, the fact Cannae was a complete victory with the wholesale annihilation of the enemy army made it the textbook example for military commanders to try to duplicate, usually, of course, without success. Cannae was the kind of annihilation that every commander from Caesar to Frederick the Great to Napoleon to Robert E. Lee sought, and that few save Caesar and Napoleon bagged whole armies is a testament as to the near impossibility of achieving a victory like Cannae.

The Battle of Cannae was an unqualified disaster for Rome, unprecedented in the annals of the city, and one with consequences which echoed around the Mediterranean. The Syracusans and Macedonians, now believing that Rome's star was on the wane, abandoned their alliances with the Republic and sided instead with Hannibal. With yet another Roman army decimated, Rome was again at Hannibal's mercy, as Livy noted: "Never before, while the City itself was still safe, had there been such excitement and panic within its walls. I shall not attempt to describe it, nor will I weaken the reality by going into details... it was not wound upon wound but multiplied disaster that was now announced. For according to the reports two consular armies and two consuls were lost; there was no longer any Roman camp, any general, any single soldier in existence; Apulia, Samnium, almost the whole of Italy lay at Hannibal's feet. Certainly there is no other nation that would not have succumbed beneath such a weight of calamity."

In just 20 months, Hannibal had destroyed three Roman armies, totaling about 16 legions and upwards of 150,000-200,000 men, and it is estimated that Rome had lost 20% of its adult men. Once again, however, Hannibal inexplicably wavered and opted not to attack Rome itself. Though he still lacked siege equipment, there would almost certainly have been someone among his allies with expertise in siege warfare, but Hannibal refused to march north, choosing instead to stay in southern Italy. Much of the blame for Hannibal's supineness, in this case, remains with the Carthaginian oligarchy, who once again refused to provide him with money, reinforcements, or the siege equipment he so vitally needed. According to legend, after Cannae the Numidian cavalry commander Maharbal suggested that Hannibal march on Rome. When Hannibal resisted, Maharbal was alleged to have said, "Truly the Gods have not bestowed all things upon the same person. Thou knowest indeed, Hannibal, how to conquer, but thou knowest not how to make use of your victory."

Hannibal followed this victory, a "disaster for Rome memorable as few others have been," with an even greater slaughter at the Battle of Cannae the following year. Despite being outnumbered by the Romans, who fielded over 86,000 men to Hannibal's 50,000, Hannibal again succeeded in bringing superior tactics to the field, stretching his line and enveloping the densely massed Romans. Though they soon knew they would be defeated, most of the Romans stood their ground with Consul Lucius Aemilius Paullus, and fought desperately to the end. "Men preferred to die where they stood rather than flee, and the victors, furious at them for delaying the victory, butchered without mercy those whom they could not dislodge… at Cannae hardly fifty men shared the consul's flight, nearly the whole army met their death in company with the other consul."[3]

Whether Hannibal made the right decision or not, he could certainly have exerted himself a little more. In the event, he chose to capture several cities in southern Italy, and established his headquarters in Capua, one of the richest cities in Southern Italy, which had defected to his side after Cannae, as had much of the southern part of the Italian Peninsula. Hannibal's lassitude during this period, referred to by classical scholars as the "lazings of Capua", is uncharacteristic, but it allowed the Romans to rally. Hannibal contented himself to send a peace delegation to negotiate terms with Rome, but the Senate still refused to deal with Hannibal. Instead, Rome re-dedicated itself to raising more armies and fighting Hannibal.

In the wake of the catastrophe at Cannae, the Roman ruling elite re-evaluated Fabius Maximus' strategy, and began to use his tactics to harass, delay, and whittle down Hannibal's forces in the field, studiously avoiding open battle whenever they could. For years they harried Hannibal's armies, and while there were blunders that allowed Hannibal to lash out (three Roman armies were destroyed in the period between 215 and 212 BCE) the victories were minor and ultimately meaningless. After almost half a decade of continuous warfare, Apulia was a scorched desert incapable of sustaining an army in the field, and Hannibal was getting no supplies either from his allies or from Carthage. Moreover, his allies were proving to be hopelessly ineffective in the field, meaning he either had to lead the force himself or risk losing one of his field armies. Whenever Hannibal did take command, the results were often devastating for Rome, but decisive victory eluded him. Rome could raise far more troops than Hannibal, unsupported, could ever

---

[3] Livy, 22.49-22.50

hope to obtain, and a war of attrition was destined to favor them in the end. The tide was finally turning against Hannibal.

Hannibal's decision not to march on Rome itself has befuddled historians for generations, and it even became a popular oration topic for Roman boys in the immediate centuries to follow, According to Livy, this fact was even remarked upon by Maharbal, the commander of Hannibal's allied Numidian cavalry, who urged Hannibal to march onto Rome. "That you may know," he said to Hannibal, "what has been gained by this battle I prophesy that in five days you will be feasting as victor in the Capitol. Follow me; I will go in advance with the cavalry; they will know that you are come before they know that you are coming." To Hannibal the victory seemed too great and too joyous for him to realize all at once. He told Maharbal that he commended his zeal, but he needed time to think out his plans. Maharbal replied, "The gods have not given all their gifts to one man. You know how to win victory, Hannibal, you do not how to use it." Livy further credits the day of delay as having saved the Roman Republic from certain disaster.[4]

What did cause Hannibal's delay? Was it simply a case of sloth? Was he actually emotionally overwhelmed as suggested by Livy? Roman historians play up Hannibal's deep hatred of Rome as the driving force behind his invasion, and while he almost certainly held no great love for the Republic, the abiding hatred may be an exaggeration. Hannibal was a general first and foremost, and his object was to win the war. He also maintained a Hellenistic viewpoint on war, believing that war was mainly a political tool that could be won by demonstrating superiority in multiple battles. In essence, he may have believed the way to an ultimate end of the war was to make clear that the other side had no reason to keep fighting, and therefore bring the enemy to the table for peace negotiations. Hannibal also hoped that his major victories would draw tribes allied with Rome to abandon their agreements and to throw their support behind his efforts.

It is important to remember that to a certain degree, he was correct. Many northern Italian tribes were glad to support his cause, and King Philip of Macedonia also pledged his support, kicking off the Macedonian Wars with Rome. Yet Hannibal had greatly misunderstood Roman culture and tenacity in his calculations, and he apparently did not grasp the Roman style of warfare. Rome did not see war as a basic tool to settle mild political disagreements, but as a method of total subjugation. They would not yield until completely dominated or destroyed. Additionally, though many of the tribes and nations bound to Rome were only attached through feeble political ties, the tribes of the Latins and Sabines closer to the Roman heartland were deeply connected to the Romans through their shared lineage, history, and mythology. Hannibal had seriously miscalculated if he expected Rome's staunchest allies to abandon them.

Hannibal himself may have realized his mistake in the weeks and months following Cannae, when despite his devastating victories, only a few tribes defected to his cause and the Romans

---

[4] Livy, 22.51

staunchly refused to enter into peace negotiations. Their reputation for stubborn willpower was no idle boast. Livy claimed that Hannibal eventually realized his error, and that when the Carthaginian Senate recalled him back to Africa, he called down "curses on his own head for not having led his armies straight to Rome when they were still bloody from the victorious field of Cannae." The Senate would prove to be a stumbling block for Hannibal as well. While Hannibal pushed the direct approach in the hopes to conclude a lucrative peace, the Senate remained heavily focused on regaining the territories they had lost to the Romans – their goal from the outset of the war. Hannibal could have aided this cause by a direct march on Rome, as Rome would have been forced to recall some of their legions occupying these outlying territories, thus opening the regions to Carthaginian attack. Yet Hannibal failed to see this course of action, and after Cannae, as it became clear that the Romans would not be willing to negotiate, the Carthaginian Senate became lukewarm in their support of Hannibal.[5]

Ironically, the Carthaginian Senate was likely to blame for what may have been more personal reasons that Hannibal did not press his attack on Rome, and why he would eventually struggle when faced with Roman legions under the command of a competent battlefield leader in the person of Publius Cornelius Scipio. In Carthage, generals were at risk of severe punishment if they experienced failure, anything from heavy fines to exile to crucifixion. An admiral by the name of Hanno suffered the latter for his failures in the First Punic War, and several defeated Carthaginian generals committed suicide rather than face punishment. While this fear provided high motivation for success, it also led many Carthaginian generals to be overcautious in battle, to the heavy advantage of an opposing commander able to commit without hesitation.[6]

Despite all of the various factors at play, Hannibal's decision may be no more complicated than a strategic weighing of his resources and the difficulty of the task before him. Cannae was hardly a short march from Rome; in fact, it was a distance of almost 250 miles. Although there was no chance that Rome could muster up a force large enough to meet the Carthaginians in open battle, a siege is an entirely different proposition. A much smaller group of soldiers, likely aided by the citizens of the city, can hold out in a siege of a walled city against a larger foe, using the defenses to their advantage. At the time of the Punic War, siege assaults were relatively new. Prior to the rise of the Macedonian Empire, sieges were generally lengthy affairs, intended to last for months or even years until the city was finally forced to open their gates due to starvation. Philip II of Macedonia, however, embraced the development of siege engines and tactics to actually assault and breach a city's walls, an art that his son Alexander the Great then perfected. A siege assault was certainly a possibility for Hannibal, but it would be terribly costly in resources and lives.[7]

Even using assault tactics, it was likely to last a long time, increasing the casualties and putting

---

⁵ Livy, 30.20
⁶ Hoyos, *The Carthaginians*, p. 35-36
⁷ Goldsworthy, 215

the Carthaginian army in a precarious logistical position, exposed on the tip of their supply lines and vulnerable to a return of Roman legions posted in foreign regions. It is conceivable that Hannibal could not have even managed to take the city in a protracted siege and that if the Romans mounted a defense, he would have been stopped at the walls. Most states in a similar situation to Rome would have capitulated under the pressure of the threat, but, as Adrian Goldsworthy noted, "on other occasions the Romans endured great defeats without ever losing their belief in ultimate victory…Certainly, if any state could have coped with such pressure, then it was Rome."[8]

That said, even if Rome was perhaps best suited to stand firm against overwhelming odds, it is impossible to state definitively that the Romans would have stalwartly refused peace negotiations in the face of a full-scale Carthaginian siege. That moment marked the best hope for a Carthaginian victory in the Second Punic War, and the likely subsequent shift in the trajectory of history. Had they sued for peace, Rome would have been hit with war indemnities and losses of territory as Carthage had been in the First Punic War, interrupting its steady rise to power. At the time of the Second Punic War and Hannibal's march through Italy, Rome was engaged in other conflicts and disputes to the east as well, including the First Macedonian War and multiple entreaties for aid from Hellenistic allies, including its long-time ally Pergamon. In the coming years, Rome would receive more calls for assistance from the Mediterranean states. The rising role of requested arbitrator was one of the things that placed Rome in a commanding position to help conquer and consolidate its empire, and that simply would not have occurred had Rome lost the Second Punic War to the Carthaginians when Hannibal was positioned to strike a blow against the city itself.

War in Africa

In 211, Hannibal received a massive blow as, while his army was in the field, the Romans besieged and captured, with great loss, his base at Capua. Still reeling from this news, his woes were compounded when he discovered that his Syracusan allies had also been crushed, with Sicily fallen to the Romans, and Philip, the king of Macedon, also defeated and driven out of the Roman dominions. Hannibal himself continued to prove himself a great general, inflicting several notable defeats upon all the armies sent against him, but they were, in the long term, meaningless. He fought on, but continued to lose territories throughout 210 and 209 BCE, and between 208 and 207 BCE he was pushed ever southwards, finally being forced to retire to Apulia, where he anxiously awaited reinforcements under the command of his brother, Hasdrubal. At the eleventh hour, these reinforcements might have turned the tide, for once he had the troops at his command Hannibal planned to march upon Rome once and for all. However, Hasdrubal never reached Hannibal. He got himself entangled in a battle with the Romans on the Metaurus, and his army was defeated and he himself killed. Hannibal, knowing his situation in Apulia was untenable, was forced to retreat into Bruttium, the southernmost tip of

---

[8] Goldsworthy, 216

the Italian peninsula, where he was also forced to endure the horror of having his brother's severed head tossed over the walls and into his camp.

For all intents and purposes, Hannibal's campaign in Italy was over. He succeeded in holding on in Bruttium for a further four years, but he was never able to push northward and his army was fast dwindling to nothing, with his veterans being killed off and his mercenaries melting away. In 206 BCE, it was reported to him that Roman armies had occupied the entirety of Iberia, driving the Carthaginian forces from the peninsula, a victory obtained by his old enemy Scipio Africanus, who had utterly crushed the Carthaginians at Ilipa. Finally, in 203 BCE, he was peremptorily recalled to Carthage, 15 years and scores of victories after he had first entered Italy in arms. The reason for his recall was simple: Rome was on the march. A massive army, under the command of Scipio Africanus, the general whose bravery had saved his eponymous father's life at the beginning of Hannibal's Italian campaign, was preparing to attack and destroy Carthage. Rome wanted revenge.

A statue depicting Hannibal, with the rings of the Roman Equestrians he had killed in the Battle of Cannae, resting on a Roman standard

While Hannibal had been in Italy, it had been relatively easy for the Carthaginian oligarchy, particularly the Hundred and Four, a federation of powerful traders, and Hannibal's chief political rival, Hanno the Great, to marginalize him. For years his political party, the Barcids, had struggled to obtain even a token amount of funds and troops for his enterprise, but Hannibal's arrival on the scene changed all that. Even his rivals could not deny the simple fact that, all else aside, the man could fight a battle like no other general alive. With Rome threatening invasion, Hannibal was suddenly the necessary hero of the hour. Bolstering his Italian mercenaries with levies from Africa and Carthage, the Carthaginian ruling elite desperately invested the money that Hannibal had begged for throughout the last decade in order to assemble a scratch force capable of at least presenting an appearance of force against Scipio Africanus' army.

Hannibal can hardly have been thrilled to see the amount of trouble the Carthaginians went to in order to assemble an army that, had he had his way years before, might well have been completely unnecessary. Certainly it appears that he prepared to take the field with less than his customary ardor. At 45, he was still far from old, but ever since he had first left Carthage he had spent virtually all of his adult life fighting, and the strain was beginning to tell. By all accounts he was in poor health, and prone to sickness. Indeed, rather than seek to bring Scipio Africanus to battle, in 202 BCE Hannibal met the Roman general and attempted to talk peace. The army the Carthaginians had succeeded in gathering, not to mention the presence of Hannibal himself, convinced Scipio that he might be well-advised to seek a diplomatic solution, and the two began negotiations, which were helped by the fact that both generals recognized a kindred spirit in the other. Through negotiations, Carthage was forced to give up much, especially considering Hannibal's roster of victories, but Rome's star was on the rise once again, and Hannibal knew he could not hope to win a protracted war.

Hannibal agreed to Scipio's terms: Carthage would lose possession of Iberia and the Mediterranean islands, renouncing all claims to overseas territories but maintaining its heartland and African possessions, with the exception of the Numidian kingdom of Masinissa, who had declared for Rome. Reparations would be made, Scipio demanded, to Rome itself and to the countless families which Carthage's wars had decimated, and the Carthaginian army and fleet must both be reduced in numbers, in order for them to never again threaten Rome's supremacy. Hannibal, who recognized these terms, though harsh, as probably the best deal Carthage was likely to achieve, acceded to them, but the proposed peace between he and Scipio never happened. While the negotiations were going on, a Roman fleet which had gotten itself stranded upon the coast of Tunisia was seized by the Carthaginian navy and ransacked of all its supplies and equipment. When Scipio heard of this, he furiously demanded reparations, but, unaccountably, the Carthaginian oligarchy high-handedly turned him down. Perhaps they felt secure enough with Hannibal at the head of an army on Carthaginian soil to defy Rome, or perhaps the terms of the treaty stung their pride. Whatever their reasons, they could not have committed a bigger diplomatic error if they had gone out of their way to do so. Scipio departed the negotiations in a rage. There would be no terms.

Engraving of the Battle of Zama

On October 19th, 202 BCE, on the plain of Zama, in modern Tunisia, battle was joined. Scipio Africanus led 34,000 Roman legionary infantry, including veteran survivors of Cannae, who had a score to settle with Hannibal, and 9,000 crack Numidian cavalry (the same heavy horse which Hannibal's general Maharbal had used to such devastating effect against the Romans for two decades). Hannibal himself marched to stop him with 45,000 Italian, Iberian, Gaulish and North African infantry (both mercenary and levied), 4,000 cavalry, and around 80 war elephants. For the first time in one of the battles of the Second Punic War, Hannibal had the infantry advantage and Rome had the cavalry advantage.

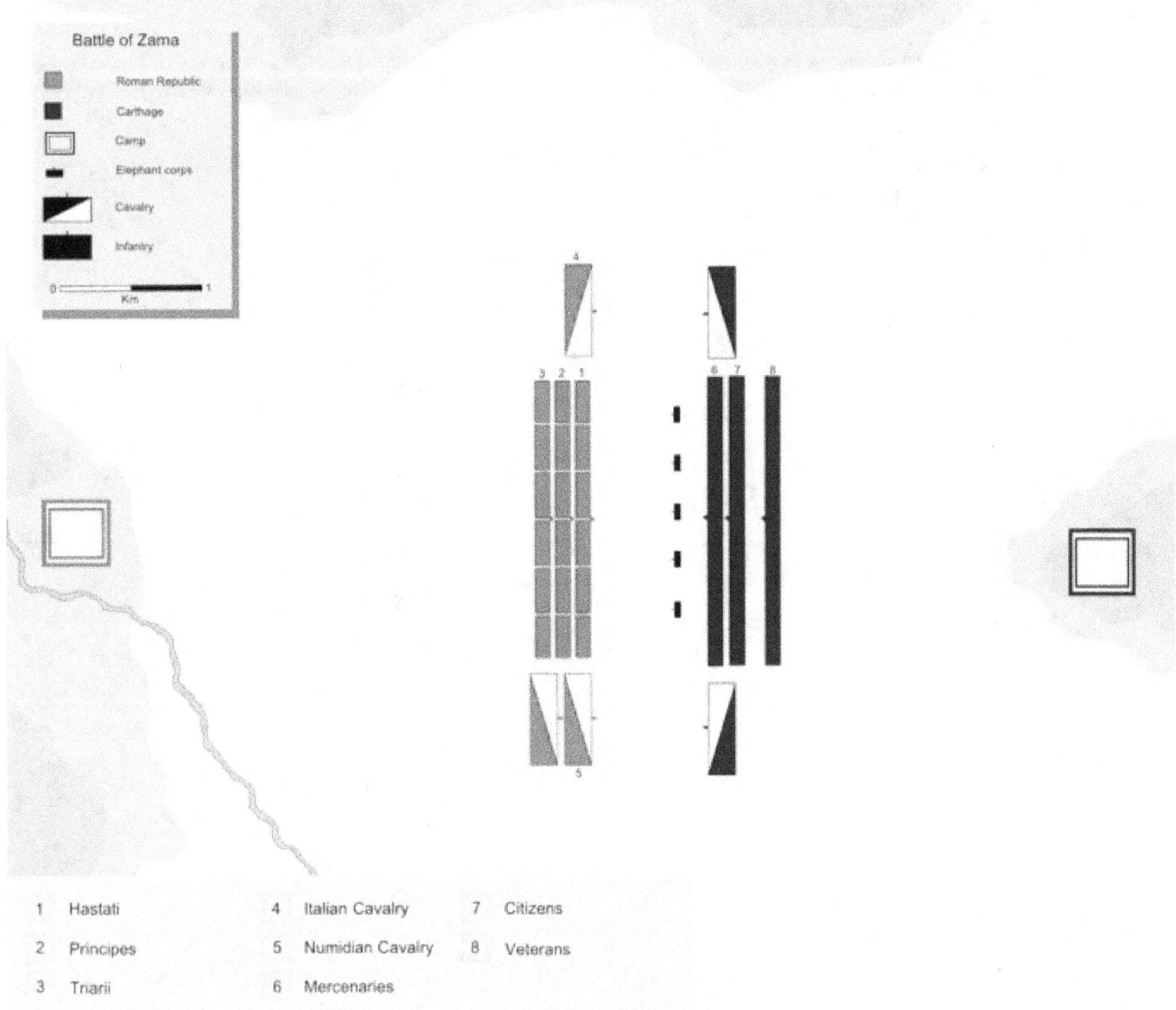

Hannibal deployed his cavalry on the wings, then placed three lines of infantry, with his Italian veterans in reserve, behind his war elephants, which were to be his secret weapon. Scipio countered by placing his own infantry in three lines, with his veteran heavy infantry in reserve and his own cavalry, which outnumbered Hannibal's by more than two to one, on the flanks. Hannibal opened the battle by pushing forward his war elephants and light infantry, but Scipio checked their advance before they could smash into his battle-lines by unleashing a cloud of skirmishers who harried the elephants with storms of arrows and javelins, while the Roman cavalry blew trumpets to confuse and frighten the elephants, several of which turned the way they had come and charged into the Carthaginian left flank, creating chaos there. Scipio also intentionally opened gaps in his own line for the elephants to drive through harmlessly. Masinissa took advantage of this to charge home against the cavalry on that flank and drive it from the field, but he found himself embroiled in a chase orchestrated on the fly by Hannibal as the Carthaginian cavalry lured him away from the main battle.

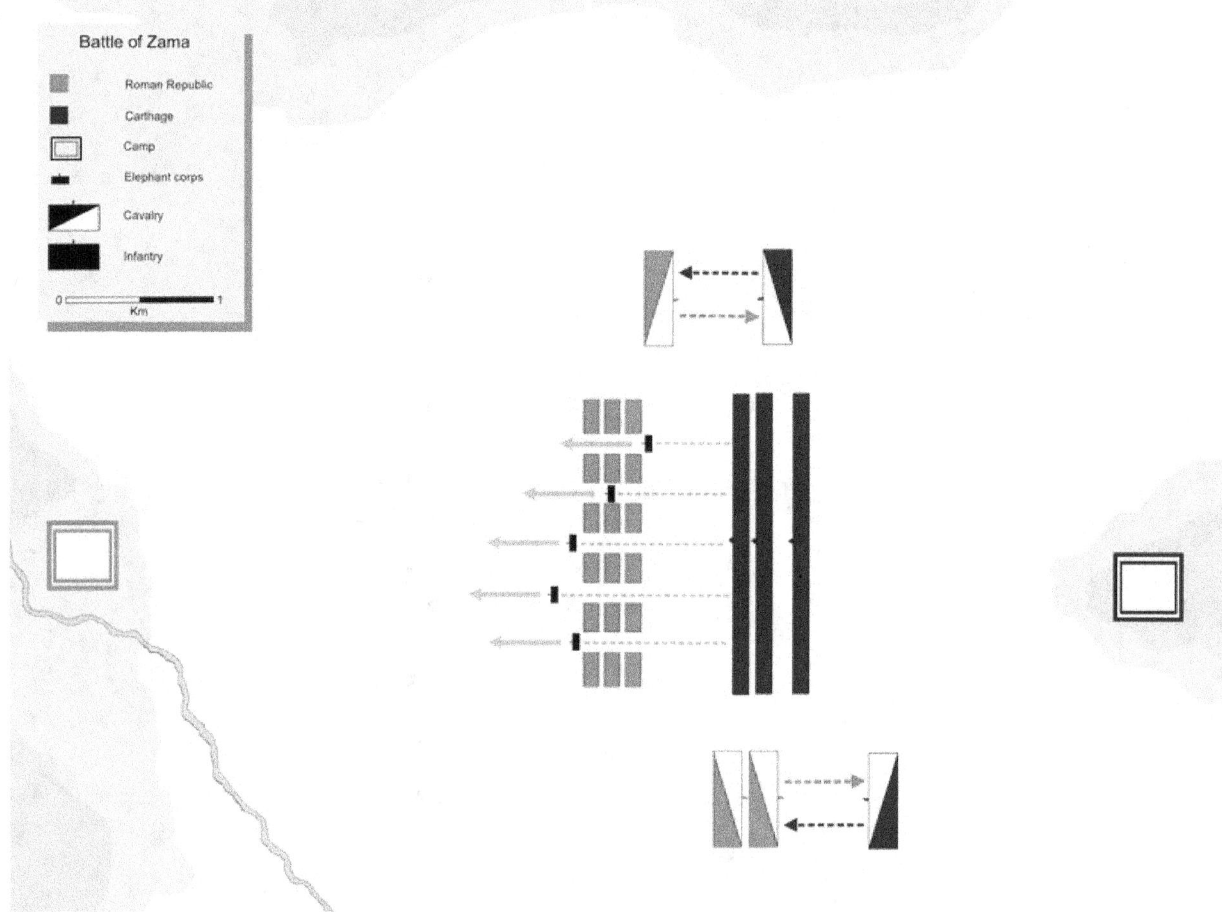

Meanwhile, the Roman and Carthaginian infantry were hammering each other in the center of the battle-line, with both sides momentarily gaining the advantage, only to be driven back in turn. The battle raged for hours, with neither side able to gain the upper hand, but eventually Masinissa, who had chased the Carthaginian cavalry clean off the field with his superior numbers, returned and charged the Carthaginian forces from behind, enveloping them. Scipio rallied his faltering and exhausted troops to one last great effort and they fell upon the Carthaginian troops, which were trapped and unable to maneuver.

Like Hannibal's masterpiece at Cannae, but this time with the roles inverted, the encircled force had nowhere to run. Thousands were cut down where they stood, with only around a tenth of Hannibal's original force, including Hannibal himself, succeeding in breaking free and escaping. For Carthage, the battle was an utter catastrophe, with over 20,000 dead and 20,000 taken prisoner, most of which were grievously wounded. Hannibal's first defeat was so dire that he lost all credibility in Carthage, and his enemies used it to blacken his reputation and forced him to surrender his generalship. With no army in the field, Carthage sued for peace, at far more costly terms than those which they could have accepted with no further loss of life.

At each of the critical points of the Battle of Zama, the fighting could just have easily swayed in favor of the Carthaginians if only certain factors had played out differently. Without the elephants taking fright at the outset of the battle, both lines of Numidian cavalry would likely have stayed on the field, not only skirmishing among themselves but also adding to the press against the military and leaving the fighting on a more even plane. Had Scipio not devised his counter-measure for the elephants, or had his soldiers not managed to execute the split-second timing successfully, the full brunt of the elephants might well have broken the Roman lines, and certainly would not have resulted in panicking the elephants and sending them back through the Carthaginian cavalry, once again giving that forward thrust to the Romans. In the same vein, without the success of both of their cavalry units, the final infantry fight could have come down to a Carthaginian victory.

If the Romans had lost the Battle of Zama, there is a good chance that the war would not have been over, but that it would eventually tip in Carthage's favor. Obviously, a loss at Zama would not have directly threatened Rome and the Romans had remained steadfastly uninterested in negotiations under heavier stress than would have than been applied. Yet the battle was decisive for the war in Africa. A loss would have left Scipio unlikely to be able to continue his campaign and forced to withdraw to Italy. Roman political favor was notoriously fickle, and their elections frequent, something that actually worked in favor of the longer-term Carthaginian generals, who enjoyed the time to learn and practice battle tactics and strategy, as well as getting to know their own men even better.

In fact, Scipio was to personally experience the fleeting nature of Roman political favor later in his own life. Jealous of his successes and frustrated with Scipio's calm, rational approach that lead to more measured peace treaties both in Carthage and in his later campaign against Antiochus of Seleucia, the Senate turned on him and his brother, accusing them without any solid proof of taking personal bribes in exchange for negotiating a more merciful truce. Though Scipio still held the love of the people and the soldiers, his bitter rivalry with the Senate caused him to retire completely from public life, and to refuse to allow his body to be buried in Rome upon his death. It is said that his gravestone read, "Thankless country, thou shalt not possess even my bones!"[9]

Failures in Africa may not have engendered the same jealousy, but very likely would have started his enmity with the Senate earlier, interrupted Scipio's career, and precluded him from further command in the now ongoing war with Carthage. As demonstrated by Hannibal's early successes and the stunning recovery of Scipio, the Roman army at the time of the Punic Wars was, in many ways, superior to that of the Carthaginians as long as it enjoyed proper leadership. The loss of Scipio in that position may have been ultimately enough to cause the Romans to lose the Second Punic War.

As with the First Punic War, the immediate effects of a loss would not have been devastating.

---

[9] Valerius Maximus, *Nine Books of Memorable Deeds and Sayings*

Although Carthage may have returned to the war in the aftermath of a victory at Zama with renewed vigor and desirous to take recompense for the damages done to African cities under their protection, it still remains unlikely that they would have utterly destroyed Rome forever. Complete annihilation of an enemy was still uncommon, and even the Romans, known for doing so, did not smash Carthage to pieces upon the resolution of the Second Punic War. Rome's fate in the case of a Carthaginian victory would likely have been similar to Carthage's, saddled once more with war debts and indemnities, and the majority of her foreign and overseas territories seized. Rome took control of the entire Iberian Peninsula and most of the islands of the Mediterranean, and her ally Masinissa was given huge swaths of territory to the west of Carthage to add to his kingdom of Numidia. Carthage was reduced to a shell of its former glory, never to rise to the level of an ancient power again.

The Third Punic War

"Moreover, they say that, shaking his gown, he took occasion to let drop some African figs before the senate. And on their admiring the size and beauty of them, he presently added, that the place that bore them was but three days' sail from Rome. Nay, he never after this gave his opinion, but at the end he would be sure to come out with this sentence, 'Also, Carthage, methinks, ought utterly to be destroyed.'" – Plutarch, *Life of Marcus Cato the Elder*

Carthage was on the brink of death, but it swiftly proved once again that it was nothing if not resourceful. Despite having been humbled and reduced virtually to city-state status, Carthage quickly recovered economically by taking advantage of the privileged trading position which had been the backbone of her wealth since her foundation. Interestingly, the ruthless demilitarization imposed by the Romans upon the Carthaginians actually aided the city's economic redevelopment; since Carthage no longer had to pay to maintain vast mercenary armies at home or abroad, their defense budget was virtually nonexistent.

Over the next five decades, Carthage slowly rebuilt her economy and even prospered, causing much annoyance and some alarm in Rome. However, ever since the defeat at Cannae, Massinissa's Numidians had raided across the new Carthaginian border with impunity, and since Carthage lacked a standing army she was forced to bring any grievances she might have before the Roman Senate, where Punic complaints were generally overruled as a matter of principle. Carthage eventually responded by refusing to pay the annual tribute to Rome and raising an army, which they launched in a retaliatory raid against Massinissa, only to promptly be defeated by the Numidians.

This behavior alarmed much of the Roman political establishment, including the famous orator Cato the Elder, who began to end all of his speeches, regardless of their subject matter, by urging the destruction of Carthage. In his biography of Cato the Elder, Plutarch wrote:

"Some will have the overthrow of Carthage to have been one of his last acts of state; when, indeed, Scipio the younger did by his velour give it the last blow, but the war, chiefly by the counsel and advice of Cato, was undertaken on the following occasion. Cato was sent to the Carthaginians and Masinissa, King of Numidia, who were at war with one another, to know the cause of their difference. He, it seems, had been a friend of the Romans from the beginning; and they, too, since they were conquered by Scipio, were of the Roman confederacy, having been shorn of their power by loss of territory and a heavy tax. Finding Carthage, not (as the Romans thought) low and in an ill condition, but well manned, full of riches and all sorts of arms and ammunition, and perceiving the Carthaginians carry it high, he conceived that it was not a time for the Romans to adjust affairs between them and Masinissa; but rather that they themselves would fall into danger, unless they should find means to check this rapid new growth of Rome's ancient irreconcilable enemy. Therefore, returning quickly to Rome, he acquainted the senate that the former defeats and blows given to the Carthaginians had not so much diminished their strength, as it had abated their imprudence and folly; that they were not become weaker, but more experienced in war, and did only skirmish with the Numidians to exercise themselves the better to cope with the Romans: that the peace and league they had made was but a kind of suspension of war which awaited a fairer opportunity to break out again.

"Moreover, they say that, shaking his gown, he took occasion to let drop some African figs before the senate. And on their admiring the size and beauty of them, he presently added, that the place that bore them was but three days' sail from Rome. Nay, he never after this gave his opinion, but at the end he would be sure to come out with this sentence, 'ALSO, CARTHAGE, METHINKS, OUGHT UTTERLY TO BE Destroyed.' But Publius Scipio Nasica would always declare his opinion to the contrary, in these words, 'It seems requisite to me that Carthage should still stand.' For seeing his countrymen to be grown wanton and insolent, and the people made, by their prosperity, obstinate and disobedient to the senate, and drawing the whole city, whither they would, after them, he would have had the fear of Carthage to serve as a bit to hold the contumacy of the multitude; and he looked upon the Carthaginians as too weak to overcome the Romans, and too great to be despised by them. On the other side, it seemed a perilous thing to Cato that a city which had been always great, and was now grown sober and wise, by reason of its former calamities, should still lie, as it were, in wait for the follies and dangerous excesses of the over-powerful Roman people; so that he thought it the wisest course to have all outward dangers removed, when they had so many inward ones among themselves.

"Thus Cato, they say, stirred up the third and last war against the Carthaginians: but no sooner was the said war begun, than he died, prophesying of the person that should put an end to it who was then only a young man"

Ancient bust of Cato the Elder

Matters ultimately did come to a head in 149 BCE, when Rome, tired of Carthaginian resurgence and seeking a pretext for invasion, first demanded that hundreds of children from Carthaginian noble families be handed over as hostages. When it seemed as though the Carthaginians might actually accede to this condition, the Romans ordered Carthage to be demolished and the entire city rebuilt inland away from the coast. The Carthaginians, unsurprisingly, told the Senate this was unacceptable, after which Rome promptly declared war.

A Roman fleet carrying 80,000 infantry and 4,000 cavalry landed in North Africa, depositing the troops near the Carthaginian city of Utica. This Roman force represented 20 legions of disciplined Roman legionaries, and they were camped only 10 miles from the city of Carthage. The presence of this force, combined with the failure of the Romans to control the Numidians and the Roman Senate's harsh demands, ensured a change in the Carthaginian government; the party which had so long sought to appease Rome following the end of the Second Punic War was replaced and a government which sought to fight the Romans and retain their Carthaginian pride came into power following the Roman demand that Carthage be abandoned.

The Roman army and fleet did not attack the Carthaginians immediately after Carthage's refusal to comply to the last demand to abandon the city, and this waiting period proved to be exceptionally costly for the Roman legions. The legions were struck down with disease, after which the combat ready legionaries were so few in number that the Roman command was unable to launch any sort of attack against the city of Carthage.

While the Roman army sough to heal itself and prepare for a vigorous campaign against Carthage, the Carthaginians were seemingly trapped within the walls of Carthage. The Romans had underestimated the tenacity of the Carthaginians, however. With 20 Roman legions a mere 10 miles from them, the Carthaginian people transformed their temples into workshops for the fabrication of weapons and armor. It was said that the Carthaginian women even went so far as to cut short their hair, and the shorn locks were twisted into cord for use as bowstrings. Thus, while the Romans sought to bring their legions back up to their peak physical condition, the Carthaginians proposed to defend themselves from the inevitable siege and gathered food and supplies.

After the passing of several months the Romans were ready to begin what they believed would be a short and successful siege. The Roman legions were divided into two commands. The first section was commanded by consul Manius Manilius, whose command consisted of the greater portion of the infantry and cavalry. His plan of attack was to cross an isthmus which separated the cities of Utica and Carthage, and upon crossing the isthmus, he would have the legions fill in the protective ditch surrounding the city of Carthage. With this impediment taken care of, he would have his legions move on to the first of two walls. The first was a low parapet which his legions would easily be able to climb, and the second was the high wall which protected the city itself. Siege engines and scaling equipment would be used to breach the high wall and attack the unprotected city.

The second wing of the Roman attack would come in the form of an attack by sea, which would be led by consul Lucius Marcius Censorinus. Censorinus would sail the Roman fleet up to the unprotected sea wall of Carthage. Some of his troops would disembark, and together the ground troops and seaborne troops would assault the city. The landed infantry and the seaborne troops would both use scaling ladders to assault the wall in conjunction with Manilius' assault on the city's front.

Once the plan of attack was agreed upon and in place, both Manius Manilius and Lucius Marcius Censorinus launched their attacks on the city. Neither of the consuls expected there to be any sort of resistance from the Carthaginians, as both men knew that the city had been unable to send out for arms, armor and assistance. Of course, both of the consuls had failed to take into consideration the fact that the Carthaginians might well have found a way to defend themselves against a Roman attack they knew was coming.

When the combined attack occurred, the consuls were horrified by the fierce, desperate resistance of the Carthaginians to the Roman attack. Confused and disorientated, the legions fell back; their first assault on Carthage had been an unequivocal failure. Having been disabused of the notion that the conquest would be easy, the consuls fell back and regrouped their forces. The consuls struck at the city once more, but again the Romans were repelled by the Carthaginians and had to fall back well away from the city.

At this point the Roman consuls became worried. Carthage would not simply surrender itself to Rome, and they were worried about forces under the Carthaginian commander Hasdrubal, who had positioned himself behind the Romans on the opposite side of a lake. He fortified his positions and looked for opportunities to strike at the Roman legions, and one came when engineers attached to Censorinus' command entered the woods around the lake. The task that they sought to accomplish was the harvesting of wood to build larger siege engines for a renewed assault upon Carthage, but while the engineers were directing the gathering of wood, a small force of Carthaginians under the command of Himilco Phameas fell upon them.

Despite the attack, the engineers, while suffering a large loss of men, were still able to gather enough wood for the siege engines, and with this wood, Censorinus and Manilius constructed new engines and ladders for a third assault upon the city of Carthage. This attack took place with both groups of legions operating in conjunction with the other, but this third attempt was still beaten back.

After this failure, Manilius focused on the fortifications in the front of the city, but even here the Carthaginians were able to successfully beat back the Roman assaults. Eventually, Manilius became despondent and lacked any belief that the Roman legions would ever succeed in breaking through the walls of Carthage.

While Manilius suffered from a lack of faith, Lucius Marius Censorinus did not. Rather than bemoaning the fate of the legions in front of Carthage, Censorinus prepared for another attempt to break into the city. Using Roman perseverance, Censorinus had his legions fill in a portion of the lake next to Carthage, and when that was done, he had a wider space with which he could assault the Carthaginian walls. Using two large battering rams, his troops finally succeeded in breaking the wall, but when they attempted to make use of the breach and gain the city, they were beaten back by the Carthaginians. When night descended, the Carthaginians started to rebuild the wall.

Although they repaired the wall, the Carthaginians also realized that the work would be insufficient to stop the Roman battering rams. What followed was an example of Carthaginian heroism and determination. Under the cover of darkness, a group of Carthaginians attacked the

Romans through the breach in the city wall in order to destroy the battering rams. The lightly armed forces were rapidly beaten back by the Roman forces, but not before disabling the battering rams and rendering them useless until the Romans could repair them.

When day dawned, the Roman legionaries saw that the Carthaginians, armed solely with clubs and stones, stood in the small courtyard open to the breach. The Carthaginians lined the courtyard, the roofs, and the walls and waited for the legionaries. The commander of the Roman troops at the breach was a young tribune by the name of Publius Cornelius Scipio Aemilianus. Instead of having his troops rush headlong into the breach, he stationed groups of men along either side of the breach and then ordered a unit of legionaries into the city.

The Carthaginians were ferocious in their defense of the city, and once again the legionaries were driven back and out of the breach. Had Aemilianus not stationed troops on either side of the breach, the Carthaginians may have succeeded in annihilating the Roman forces altogether, and as a result, Aemilianus' actions came to the attention of the commanders.

Shortly after this, before the Roman consuls could prepare the legions for another assault on Carthage, widespread illnesses began to sweep the ranks once more. With the troops sick, Censorinus took his command post out of the fleet, which sat off of the port side of Carthage, and began to plot his next move. The Carthaginians, however, had already began to act upon theirs. Since the winds were blowing towards the Roman fleet, people within the city prepared a large group of fire boats. These vessels were filled with tinder and flammables before being carried through the city to a corner of the city wall which protruded into the sea. With the wall serving as a shield from Roman eyes, the Carthaginians lowered the boats into the water and raised the sails, and as the wind started to drive the boats around the wall and towards the Roman fleet, the Carthaginians poured both pitch and brimstone onto the boats from atop the walls and lit them. The wind drove the boats furiously into the Roman ships, lighting them on fire, and the tactic proved so effective that Rome lost nearly the entire fleet anchored off of Carthage's walls.

After the loss of the fleet, Censorinus returned to Rome, both to report on the status of the war and to take care of the political necessity of conducting an election to retain his position as consul. Meanwhile, Manilius stayed within his camp outside of the city. The Carthaginians, however, did not remain within the city. Shortly after Censorius' departure for Rome the Carthaginians made a night assault upon the Roman camp. Mostly unarmed, the Carthaginian troops carried wooden planks with which to cross the ditch which surrounded the Roman camp, and after crossing the trench the Carthaginians attempted to destroy the Roman fortifications.

As the Carthaginians assaulted the front of the encampment, Aemilianus exited the camp via the rear upon his horse and charged the Carthaginians from the flank. Due to the inevitable confusion of night combat, the Carthaginians believed that the young tribune was at the head of a larger force and retreated to the sanctuary of Carthage. As the war progressed Aemilianus' name gained more recognition and renown.

Aemilianus continued making a good name for himself, and in addition to his bravery, he was known for his ability to use subterfuge and trickery when necessary. Such an incident occurred when the Carthaginians launched another attack upon Manilius' camp, this time from the sea at night. While Manilius chose to keep his troops within the walls, Aemilianus led a large group of cavalry out onto the field where the Carthaginians were gathered and assaulting the fortifications. By ordering his cavalry to carry only lit torches and to not engage the Carthaginians, and by having the cavalry ride around the enemy yelling and waving their torches, Aemilianus was able to force the Carthaginian to withdraw in confusion.

While the Carthaginians continued to hold out against the Roman siege, Manilius left his encampment with two legions to seek an engagement with a roving Carthaginian force commanded by Hasdrubal. However, Manilius' timidity and lack of tactical knowledge led him to make several poor decisions which Aemilianus attempted to turn the consul from. Undeterred, Manilius proceeded into a narrow valley, allowing Hasdrubal to ambush the two legions, but in the fighting that followed, Aemilianus took command of a large group of cavalry and effectively enabled the defeated legions to withdraw. When it was later discovered that four cohorts of the legions had been left behind, dug in yet surrounded, Aemilianus again took the initiative and with his cavalry achieved what was believed to be impossible by breaking the hold of Hasdrubal's forces around the four cohorts, driving the Carthaginians from the field, and rescuing the trapped legionaries.

Shortly after this incident, Aemilianus returned to Rome and sought out a consul seat. Many of the men with whom he had served in North Africa wrote home that Aemilianus alone could destroy Carthage. Even the consul Manilius, shortly before being replaced, sent word to Rome that Aemilianus should return to North Africa, not as a tribune but as consul, in order to bring an end to the Carthaginians.

By December of 148 BCE, the citizens of Rome had grown tired of the war already. They had also heard of Aemilianus' exploits in North Africa, so when the time to vote came, he was awarded a consul position. In addition to this, he was given North Africa as his province so that he might command the legions. The Roman public also gave him the right to conscript men into service to replace those who had already been lost in the war.

Thus, in the spring of 147 BCE, Aemilianus gathered his troops and sailed for the Carthaginian city of Utica. Meanwhile, the Romans in North Africa continued to push against the Carthaginian defenses. From the spring of 147 to the spring of 146, Aemilianus drove his forces through the Carthaginian territories, restoring discipline to the legions, capturing Carthaginian positions of strength, and stopping supplies from reaching Carthage.

Finally, as the spring of 146 neared its end, Aemilianus attacked the city of Carthage. The Carthaginians, weak from nearly three years of siege warfare, disease, and lack of supplies, were unable to defend their walls when the Romans attacked. As the legionaries poured into the city, a brutal form of fighting began from street to street and house to house. For seven days, the Romans and Carthaginians engaged in brutal urban warfare, but Rome was victorious in the end. Only 50,000 of Carthage's citizens survived, and these people were sold into slavery. For 17 days the Romans burned the city to the ground, and those buildings that remained were torn down by hand so that nothing of the city remained.

A picture of the excavated ruins of Ancient Carthage

The Roman writer Appian described the scene: "All places were filled with groans, shrieks, shouts, and every kind of agony. Some were stabbed, others were hurled alive from the roofs to the pavement, some of them alighting on the heads of spears or other pointed weapons, or swords. No one dared to set fire to the houses on account of those who were still on the roofs until Scipio reached Byrsa. Then he set fire to the three streets all together, and gave orders to keep the passageways clear of burning material so that the army might move back and forth freely. Then came new scenes of horror. As the fire spread and carried everything down, the soldiers did not wait to destroy the buildings little by little, but all in a heap. So the crashing grew louder, and many corpses fell with the stones into the midst. Others were seen still living, especially old men, women, and young children who had hidden in the inmost nooks of the houses, some of them wounded, some more or less burned, and uttering piteous cries. Still others, thrust out and falling from such a height with the stones, timbers, and fire, were torn asunder in all shapes of horror, crushed and mangled. Nor was this the end of their miseries, for the street cleaners, who were removing the rubbish with axes, mattocks, and forks, and making the roads passable, tossed with these instruments the dead and the living together into holes in the ground, dragging them along like sticks and stones and turning them over with their iron tools. Trenches were filled with men. Some who were thrown in head foremost, with their legs sticking out of the ground, writhed a long time. Others fell with their feet downward and their heads above ground. Horses ran over them, crushing their faces and skulls, not purposely on the part of the riders, but in their headlong haste. Nor did the street cleaners do these things on purpose; but the tug of war, the glory of approaching victory, the rush of the soldiery, the orders of the officers, the blast of the trumpets, tribunes and centurions marching their cohorts hither and thither - all together made everybody frantic and heedless of the spectacles under their eyes."[10]

The Third Punic War marked the end of Carthage as any sort of city or people, and it allowed Rome to continue its rise to power within the Mediterranean. Rome's ability to soundly defeat an enemy regardless of its location was a factor for new enemies and possible challengers alike to consider.

Carthage as it had existed for over half a millennium was no more. However, it soon blossomed into existence once again, albeit in a vastly different form. For a brief period, Carthage's old rival, Utica, became the hub for Roman commerce and shipping in North Africa along the route that had once made Carthage so prosperous. But eventually, the mouth of the river of Utica silted up, blocking the harbor and forcing the Romans to rebuild Carthage so they could use its anchorage safely. New Carthage quickly became one of the greatest cities in Roman North Africa, with a population of approximately half a million.

After being for years one of the most important trading hubs in the Mediterranean, Carthage later became an important theological center for the burgeoning Christian religion, and it would eventually become the capital of the Vandal Kingdom of Africa in the 5th century until it was taken by the Byzantine Empire several decades later. The city remained the capital of the Byzantine Exarchate of Africa until 698 CE, when the Arab armies of Hassan al Numan finally overran it. Al Numan founded the city of Tunis a short distance away from Carthage, and within a few years this new center had burgeoned in importance to the point that Carthage fell into ruin. Carthage would never again be a center of any great significance, and even today, it remains a suburb of Tunis.

Although the Romans suffered some minor setbacks in the outset of the Third Punic War, the conclusion of the final conflict was never likely to be any different. The pitiful state that Carthage found itself in after the Second Punic War ensured the Carthaginians no ability to defend themselves against the might of Rome alone, let alone Rome combined with the strength of its deadly Numidian allies. But had the roles been reversed and Carthage emerged triumphant

---

₁₀ Appian, 129

from the Second Punic War, would the third have ended with the compete destruction of Rome?

It may well be that the Hellenistic style of political warfare was too deeply ingrained for Carthage to have brought about the end of Rome. It is far more likely that Rome would have remained a small and relatively insignificant Italian state, never establishing the powerful empire that it eventually did. If so, would the Punic Phoenicians have managed to conquer the remainder of the Mediterranean? Would it have remained divided among numerous Hellenistic empires? The Romans certainly took heavy inspiration from the Greeks, but Hellenistic empires surviving Rome would have left an even greater Greek footprint upon the world. Perhaps the Greek language would have remained the *lingua franca* in the centuries to come. The great Ottoman Empire, which arose from the Eastern Roman Empire that later became known as the Byzantines, very likely would never have existed, and the map of Europe would have looked very different than it does today.

One would also expect significant religious differences. Without the unity of a great empire that spanned the Mediterranean and developed interconnected roads, trade systems, and travel, Christianity would likely have struggled to move so quickly through the ancient world, and left a lesser impact on the direction of European society.

Furthermore, the Romans were consummate inventors, and many of their creations remain an integral part of modern life today. Our modern calendar by which many order the year is a system adapted from the Julian calendar, which Julius Caesar introduced after his conquest of Egypt. Romans also regularized basic sanitation and advanced sewer design, something historians have considered a major indicator of the success of ancient nations. They developed interconnected and efficient highways and roads, apartment buildings to maximize use of space in urban locations, an organized postal service, aqueducts and indoor plumbing systems, and even indoor heating and furnace systems. The grid pattern that they used for the organization of their cities remains common in many cities around the world today, and basic architectural tenets commonplace today, such as arches for improved stability, were first introduced in Rome. Certain Roman inventions also remain a part of daily existence, including books and newspapers, concrete, and precision surgical tools.

In addition to being some of the longest lasting and most deadly wars in antiquity, the fact that the belligerents were the two most powerful states in the Mediterranean meant that the Punic Wars could not help but to be a defining moment in history. And while it is often forgotten today, the results of the first two wars defined the shape of history. On numerous occasions, a mistake, a twist of fortune, a change in timing, or a single different individual could have swung the pendulum and changed the outcome of the fighting, thereby altering the trajectory of Western Civilization.

Online Resources

Other books about ancient history by Charles River Editors

Further Reading

Bagnall, Nigel (1990). The Punic Wars. ISBN 0-312-34214-4.

Goldsworthy, Adrian (2006). The Fall of Carthage. ISBN 978-03043-6642-2.

Lazenby, John Francis (1978). Hannibal's War. ISBN 978-0-8061-3004-0.

Lancel, Serge (1995). Hannibal (in French).

Polybius, Histories, Evelyn S. Shuckburgh (translator); London, New York. Macmillan (1889); Reprint Bloomington (1962).

Palmer, Robert E. A. (1997). Rome and Carthage at Peace. Stuttgart.

Barceló, Pedro A. (1988). Karthago und die iberische Halbinsel vor den Barkiden: Studien zur karthagischen Präsenz im westlichen Mittelmeerraum von der Gründung von Ebusus bis zum Übergang Hamilkars nach Hispanien (in German). Bonn. ISBN 3-7749-2354-X.

Ameling, Walter (1993). Karthago: Studien zu Militär, Staat und Gesellschaft (in German). Munich. ISBN 3-406-37490-5.

Zlattner, Max (1997). Hannibals Geheimdienst im Zweiten Punischen Krieg (in German). Konstanz. ISBN 3-87940-546-8.

Mahaney, W.C, 2008. "Hannibal's Odyssey, Environmental Background to the Alpine Invasion of Italia," Gorgias Press, Piscataway, N.J, 221 pp.

Dodge, Theodore Ayrault (1891). Hannibal. Reprinted by Da Capo Press, Cambridge, Mass. ISBN 0-306-81362-9

Free Books by Charles River Editors

We have brand new titles available for free most days of the week. To see which of our titles are currently free, click on this link.

Discounted Books by Charles River Editors

We have titles at a discount price of just 99 cents everyday. To see which of our titles are currently 99 cents, click on this link.